HAMLYN POCKET GUIDES

SPANISH

PHRASE BOOK
AND DICTIONARY

HAMLYN POCKET GUIDES

SPANISH

PHRASE BOOK
AND DICTIONARY

compiled by

LEXUS

with Aurora Luelmo
and Dorothy Anne O'Neill

First published 1989 by
The Hamlyn Publishing Group Limited
Michelin House, 81 Fulham Road
LONDON SW3 6RB

Second impression 1989

ISBN 0 600 56431 2

Printed in Great Britain

INTRODUCTION

This new phrase book and dictionary has been designed to combine a large number of features in a single integrated package.

A total of 101 concise sections, arranged in alphabetical order, give you information on how to deal with a variety of situations in Spanish. Flicking through the book and looking at the headings at the tops of the pages will give you an instant guide to the contents list.

There are sections for activities such as shopping, driving, changing money, buying a ticket, ordering a meal etc.

There are sections which enable you to express reactions, to express your feelings, likes, dislikes, emotions etc. Sections for making requests, for talking about yourself and for understanding people.

And the nuts and bolts of the language are clearly presented in straightforward grammar sections so that you can go further with your Spanish and develop some skill in the language.

And for deciphering Spanish signs a comprehensive list of things you're likely to see when travelling abroad has been included — in addition to a menu reader and drinks list. And as well as this a number of typical responses that you might get from Spanish people if you say something or ask a question in Spanish have been included.

All the phrases are provided with an easy-to-use pronunciation guide (see below) and there are also guidelines on the pronunciation of Spanish.

And so that you can build up your Spanish vocabulary and make modifications to the phrases given in the various sections, this book also includes a 3,000 word dictionary of English into Spanish.

Some notes on the pronunciation system used

The pronunciation guide in this book is based on writing out Spanish words as though they were English words. So if you read out the pronunciation line as English you will communicate with a Spanish person. (For more information on Spanish pronunciation, see *PRONUNCIATION*). Some special conventions have been used.

H	like the ch sound in the Scottish pronunciation of 'loch'
ī	like the i sound in 'tie' or 'cry'
th	as in 'theatre'

Letters in bold print in the pronunciation guide show which part of a word is to be stressed.

Notes on translation

When the word 'you' has been given two translations, the first is the familiar **tú** form and the second the polite **usted** form. Where there is only one translation for 'you' this will be the polite form. For more on this see PRONOUNS.

An **a** in brackets indicates the feminine form of a word (*see ADJECTIVES*).

ACCEPTING, SAYING YES

Yes please.
Sí, gracias.
see grath-yas

Thank you.
Gracias.
grath-yas

Please.
Por favor.
por favor

Yes, I'd like to.
Sí, encantado(a).
see enkantado(a)

Yes, that would be very nice.
Sí, me gustaría mucho.
see meh goostaree-a moocho

Ok, fine.
Vale, bien.
baleh b-yen

I'd love one, I'd love to.
Con mucho gusto.
kon moocho goosto

I'll take two.
Cojeré dos.
koнereh dos

That's just right thanks.
Así está bien, gracias.
asee esta b-yen grath-yas

Great!, good idea!
¡Estupendo!, ¡qué buena idea!
estoopendo keh bwena eedeh-a

ADJECTIVES

Adjectives in Spanish have to 'agree' with the noun they qualify. The form of the adjective changes according to whether the noun it describes is masculine, feminine, singular or plural.

The feminine is formed in the following way:

Change the masculine endings	**-o**		**-a**
	-or	to	**-ora**
	-és		**-esa**

Un chico tonto.
oon cheeko tonto
A silly boy.

Una chica tonta.
oona cheeka tonta
A silly girl.

Un sitio encantador.
oon seet-yo enkantador
A lovely place.

Una persona encantadora.
oona pairsona enkantadora
A lovely person.

Un hombre aragonés.
oon ombreh aragones
A man from Aragon.

Una mujer aragonesa.
oona mooнair aragonesa
A woman from Aragon.

In most other cases, the feminine forms are the same as the masculine:

Un hombre difícil.
oon ombreh deefeetheel
A difficult man.

Una lección difícil.
oona lekth-yon deefeetheel
A difficult lesson.

Note that, unlike in English, Spanish adjectives are normally placed *after* the noun.

The plurals of adjectives in Spanish are formed in the same way as the plurals of nouns (i.e. by adding **-s**):

Una casa grande.
oona kasa grandeh
A big house.

Muchas casas grandes.
moochas kasas grandes
A lot of big houses.

AGREEING WITH PEOPLE

That's right.
Exactamente.
exaktamenteh

No, no, you're quite right.
No, no, tienes/tiene toda la razón.
no no t-yenes/t-yeneh toda la rathon

Oh yes.
Ah, sí.
a see

That's just what I think.
Eso creo yo.
eso kreh-o yo

Absolutely.
Desde luego.
dezdeh lwehgo

You were right.
Tenías/tenía razón.
tenee-as/tenee-a rathon

That's true, true enough.
Es verdad.
es bairdad

He agrees with me.
Está de acuerdo conmigo.
esta deh akwairdo konmeego

Me too/neither do I.
Yo también/yo tampoco.
yo tamb-yen/yo tampoko

> **Eso es.**
> *eso es*
> That's it.

ALPHABET

The alphabet in Spanish is pronounced as follows:

a *ah*
b *beh*
c *theh*
ch *chech*
d *deh*
e *eh*
f *efeh*
g *Heh*
h *acheh*
i *ee*
j *Hota*
k *kah*
l *eleh*
ll *e(l)yeh*
m *emeh*
n *eneh*
ñ *en-yeh*
o *oh*
p *peh*
q *koo*
r, rr *ereh, erreh*
s *esseh*
t *teh*
u *oo*
v *oobeh*
w *oobeh-dobleh*
x *ekees*
y *ee gr-yehga*
z *thehta*

To spell your name, Harris, in Spanish you would say:
acheh-ah-ereh-ereh-ee-esseh

See also the section on PRONUNCIATION.

ANNOYANCE

Bother! Damn!
¡Porras! ¡Puñetas!
porras poon-yehtas

It's very annoying.
Es muy molesto.
es mwee molesto

That's totally impossible.
Eso es totalmente imposible.
eso es totalmenteh eemposeebleh

Don't be silly.
No seas tonto.
no seh-as tonto

Rubbish!
¡Tonterías!
tonteree-as

Of course not!
¡Claro que no!
klaro keh no

What do you expect!
¡Pues qué te esperas!
pwehs keh teh espairas

Oh come on now!
¡Venga ya!
ben-ga ya

You idiot!
¡Idiota!
eed-yota

11

APOLOGIES

Sorry.
¡Perdón!
pairdon

I'm very sorry.
¡Lo siento mucho!
lo s-yento moocho

RESPONSES

No se preocupe.
no seh preh-okoopeh
Don't worry.

Nada, nada.
nada nada
That's ok.

No tiene importancia.
no t-yeneh eemportanth-ya
It doesn't matter.

He says he's very sorry.
Dice que lo siente mucho.
deetheh keh lo s-yenteh moocho

Please accept my apologies.
Le ruego me disculpe.
leh rwehgo meh deeskoolpeh

I feel awful.
Lo siento horrores.
lo s-yento orrores

I'll buy you another one.
Yo le compro otro.
yo leh kompro otro

12

ARTICLES

The definite article (the), has various forms in Spanish, which depend on the number and gender of the noun it introduces.

	singular	*plural*
masculine	**el**	**los**
feminine	**la**	**las**

El coche/los coches.
el kocheh/los koches
The car/the cars.

La mesa/las mesas.
la mehsa/las mehsas
The table/the tables.

The article **el**, when used in combination with **a** (to) or **de** (of), undergoes the following changes:

a + el = al
de + el = del

Vamos al parque.
bamos al parkeh
We're going to the park.

Cerca del cine.
thairka del theeneh
Near the cinema.

The indefinite article (a, an, some), also varies according to whether the noun is masculine, feminine, singular or plural:

	singular	plural
masculine	un	unos
feminine	una	unas

Un amigo.
oon ameego
A friend.

Unos amigos.
oonos ameegos
Some friends.

Una silla.
oona see-ya
A chair.

Unas sillas.
oonas see-yas
Some chairs.

ATTENTION: GETTING PEOPLE'S ATTENTION

Excuse me!
¡Por favor!
por favor

Hello!
¡Oiga!
oyga

Waiter!
¡Camarero!
kamarehro

Waitress!
¡Camarera!
kamarehra

Miss!
¡Señorita!
sen-yoreeta

Is there anyone there?
¿Hay alguien ahí?
i alg-yen a-ee

Hoy you!
¡Oye, tú!
oyeh too

> **¡Señor!**
> *sen-yor*
> Excuse me (sir)!

> **¡Señora!**
> *sen-yora*
> Excuse me (madam)!

BANKS

Can I change this into pesetas?
¿Puedo cambiar esto en pesetas?
pwehdo kamb-yar esto en pesehtas

I want to draw cash on this credit card.
Quiero sacar dinero con esta tarjeta de crédito.
k-yehro sakar deenehro kon esta tarнehta deh krehdeeto

I'd like to cash these traveller's cheques.
Querría canjear estos cheques de viaje.
keh-reea kanнeh-ar estos chekehs deh b-yaнeh

Can I cash this cheque here?
¿Puedo cobrar este cheque aquí?
pwehdo kobrar esteh chekeh akee

This is the phone number of my bank in England/Scotland.
Este es el teléfono de mi banco en Inglaterra/Escocia.
esteh es el telefono deh mee banko en eenglaterra/eskoth-ya

RESPONSES

¿Me permite el pasaporte?
meh pairmeeteh el pasaporteh
Can I have your passport?

Recoja su dinero en la ventanilla de pagos.
rekoнa soo deenehro en la bentaneeya deh pagos
You get your money at the cash desk.

Can you give me some small change as well?
¿Me puede dar también algo suelto?
meh pwehdeh dar tamb-yen algo swelto

Can you change this into smaller notes?
¿Me puede cambiar esto en billetes más pequeños?
meh pwehdeh kamb-yar esto en bee-yeнtes mas pekehn-yos

BE: THE VERB TO BE

'To be' can be translated by two different verbs in Spanish — **SER** and **ESTAR**. The forms are:

SER

soy	*soy*	I am	**somos**	*somos*	we are
eres	*eres*	you are	**sois**	*soys*	you are
es	*es*	he/she/it is	**son**	*son*	they are

ESTAR

estoy	*estoy*	I am	**estamos**	*estamos*	we are
estás	*estas*	you are	**estáis**	*estís*	you are
está	*esta*	he/she/it is	**están**	*estan*	they are

SER indicates an inherent quality, a permanent state or characteristic, something which is unlikely to change:

> **It's a big world.**
> El mundo es grande.
> *el moondo es grandeh*

The world has always been big, and is unlikely to be anything else but big.

> **Ice is cold.**
> El hielo es frío.
> *el yehlo es free-o*

SER is also used with occupations, nationalities, the time and to indicate possession:

> **My mother is Spanish.**
> Mi madre es española.
> *mee madreh es espan-yola*

> **My brother is a doctor.**
> Mi hermano es médico.
> *mee airmano es mehdeeko*

The dog's mine.
El perro es mío.
el perro es mee-o

It's two o'clock in the morning.
Son las dos de la madrugada.
son las dos deh la madroogada

ESTAR, on the other hand, is used for temporary qualities, for things which could change:

We are very happy.
Estamos muy contentos.
estamos mwee kontentos

This pear isn't ripe.
Esta pera no está madura.
esta paira no esta madoora

The water's warm.
El agua está caliente.
el agwa esta kal-yenteh

Notice the difference between the following two phrases:

Soy una persona alegre.
soy oona pairsona alegreh
I am a cheerful person. (of a cheerful nature)

Mi amiga está alegre (hoy).
mee ameega esta alegreh (oy)
My friend is cheerful (today).

ESTAR is also used to indicate position:

The Prado is in Madrid.
El Prado está en Madrid.
el prado esta en madreed

BEACH, THE POOL

Let's go down to the beach.
¡Vamos a la playa!
bamos a la plīya

I'm going to the pool.
Voy a la piscina.
boy a la peestheena

They're on the beach.
Están en la playa.
estan en la plīya

Can we have a beach umbrella?
¿Podemos coger una sombrilla?
podehmos koнair oona sombreeya

Where do you get the towels from?
¿Dónde se cogen las toallas?
dondeh se koнen las to-a-yas

Can I have a recliner?
¿Puedo coger una hamaca?
pwehdo koнair oona amaka

Are you coming in?
¿Te vienes/se viene al agua?
teh b-yenes/seh b-yeneh al agwa

I can't swim.
No sé nadar.
no seh nadar

> **Prohibido bañarse.**
> *pro-eebeedo ban-yarseh*
> No bathing.

BUSES

Which bus goes to …?
¿Qué autobús va a …?
keh owtoboos ba a

Does this bus go to …?
¿Va este autobús a …?
ba esteh owtoboos a

When's the next bus to …?
¿A qué hora es el próximo autobús a …?
a keh ora es el proxeemo owtoboos a

Is there a bus that goes there?
¿Hay algún autobús que vaya para allá?
i algoon owtoboos keh biya para a-ya

What time does the bus go back?
¿A qué hora es el autobús de vuelta?
a keh ora es el owtoboos deh bwelta

When does the last bus leave?
¿A qué hora sale el último autobús?
a keh ora saleh el oolteemo owtoboos

A single to …
Un billete de ida a …
oon beeyehteh deh eeda a

Two returns to …
Dos billetes de ida y vuelta a …
dos beeyehtes deh eeda ee bwelta a

Could you tell me when to get off?
¿Me puede decir cuándo me tengo que bajar?
meh pwehdeh detheer kwando meh ten-go keh baнar

> **Parada de autobús.**
> *parada deh owtoboos*
> Bus stop.

BUSINESS TRAVEL

I'm here on business.
Estoy aquí en viaje de negocios.
estoy akee en b-yaHeh deh negoth-yos

James O'Connor to see Mr ...
Por favor, dígale al señor ... que está aquí James
O'Connor.
*por favor deegaleh al sen-yor ... keh esta akee James
O'Connor*

My company is ...
Mi empresa es ...
mee emprehsa es

I'll wait.
Esperaré.
esperareh

Do you have a card?
¿Tiene usted tarjeta?
t-yeneh oostehd tarHehta

We'd like to get this firmed up.
Nos gustaría dejar esto solucionado.
nos goostaree-a deHar esto solooth-yonado

Can you give us more time?
¿Puede darnos un plazo más largo?
pwehdeh darnos oon platho mas largo

I'll get them faxed over.
Los enviaré por fax.
los emb-yareh por fax

It's a pleasure doing business with you.
Es un placer tratar de negocios con usted.
es oon plathair tratar deh negoth-yos kon oostehd

CAMPING

Excuse me, do you know where the nearest campsite is?
Por favor, ¿sabe usted por dónde queda el camping más cercano?
por favor sabeh oostehd por dondeh kehda el kampeeng mas thairkano

Can we camp here?
¿Podemos acampar aquí?
podehmos akampar akee

Can you give us a camping pass?
¿Nos puede dar un pase para el camping?
nos pwehdeh dar oon paseh para el kampeeng

How much is it per night?
¿Cuál es el precio por noche?
kwal es el preth-yo por nocheh

We'd like to stay one night/two nights/a week.
Querríamos quedarnos una noche/dos noches/una semana.
keh-reeamos kehdarnos oona nocheh/dos noches/oona semana

Is this drinking water?
Este agua ¿es potable?
esteh agwa es potableh

Do you sell calor gas?
¿Tiene camping gas?
t-yeneh kampeeng gas

Which way to the shops?
¿Por dónde se va a las tiendas?
por dondeh seh ba a las t-yendas

Do you have a map with campsites on it?
¿Tiene un mapa de campings?
t-yeneh oon mapa deh kampeengs

CAR ACCIDENTS

He came straight out.
Se atravesó de repente.
seh atrabeso deh repenteh

He didn't look.
No miró.
no meero

She was going far too fast.
Iba a mucha velocidad.
eeba a moocha belotheedad

He went through the red light.
Se saltó el semáforo.
seh salto el semaforo

He reversed into me.
Se me metió encima al dar marcha atrás.
seh meh met-yo entheema al dar marcha atras

He didn't indicate.
No puso el intermitente.
no pooso el eentermeetenteh

He was on the wrong side of the road.
Iba por el lado de la carretera que no le correspondía.
eeba por el lado deh la karretaira keh no leh korrespondee-a

Ok, it was my fault.
Vale, fue culpa mía.
baleh fweh koolpa mee-a

Did you see that?
¿Lo vio usted?
lo b-yo oostehd

Will you be a witness for me?
¿Atestiguará usted en mi favor?
atesteegwara oostehd en mee favor

Can you write down your name and address?
¿Puede escribir su nombre y dirección?
pwehdeh eskreebeer soo nombreh ee deerekth-yon

What's the name of your insurance company?
¿Cómo se llama su compañía de seguros?
komo seh yama soo kompan-yeea deh segooros

Do you want to settle this between ourselves?
¿Quiere usted que lo arreglemos entre nosotros?
k-yehreh oostehd keh lo arreglehmos entreh nosotros

Could you call the police?
¿Podría llamar a la policía?
podree-a yamar a la poleethee-a

I'm ok, I'm not hurt.
Estoy bien, no estoy herido.
estoy b-yen no estoy aireedo

She's been injured.
Está herida.
esta aireeda

Learn to drive!
¡Aprende a conducir!
aprendeh a kondootheer

CHEMIST

Is there a chemist open today?
¿Hay alguna farmacia abierta hoy?
i algoona farmath-ya ab-yairta oy

Is there a chemist open at nights?
¿Hay alguna farmacia que abra de noche?
i algoona farmath-ya keh abra deh nocheh

Have you got something for ...?
¿Tiene algo para ...?
t-yeneh algo para

Do you have something equivalent to this?
¿Tiene algo equivalente a esto?
t-yeneh algo ekeebalenteh a esto

Can you make up this prescription?
¿Puede preparar esta receta?
pwehdeh preparar esta rethehta

YOU'LL SEE

No ingerir.
no eenHereer
Not to be taken internally.

Tómese antes de las comidas.
tomeseh antes deh las komeedas
Take before meals.

Manténgase fuera del alcance de los niños.
manten-gaseh fwehra del alkantheh deh los neen-yos
Keep out of reach of children.

Farmacia de guardia.
farmath-ya deh gward-ya
Duty/all-night chemist.

CHILDREN AND BABIES

Is there a crèche?
¿Hay guardería?
i gwarderee-a

We need a baby-sitter.
Necesitamos alguien que nos cuide al niño/a los niños.
netheseetamos alg-yen keh nos kweedeh al neen-yo/a los neen-yos

We'll be back at ...
Volveremos a la/las ...
bolbairehmos a la/las

Can we have a children's portion?
¿Nos podría traer media ración para el niño/la niña?
nos podree-a tra-air mehd-ya rath-yon para el neen-yo/la neen-ya

Two adults and one child to ...
Dos billetes y uno de niño para ...
dos beeyehtes ee oono deh neen-yo para

RESPONSES

¿Cuantos años tiene?
kwantos an-yos t-yeneh
How old is he/she?

¿Qué tiempo tiene? (if talking about babies)
keh t-yempo t-yeneh
How old is he/she?

He/she is ... years/months.
Tiene ... años/meses.
t-yeneh ... an-yos/mehses

Isn't he/she lovely!
¡Qué mono/mona!
keh mono/mona

26

CINEMA AND THEATRE

Do you have a programme of what's on in town?
¿Tiene una cartelera de espectáculos?
t-yeneh oona kartelaira deh espektakoolos

I'd like to go to the cinema/theatre.
Me gustaría ir al cine/teatro.
meh goostaree-a eer al theeneh/teh-atro

I want to see a Spanish film/play.
Quiero ver una película/obra de teatro española.
k-yehro bair oona peleekoola/obra deh teh-atro espan-yola

Can I book two seats for this evening?
¿Podría reservar dos localidades para esta tarde/noche?
podree-a reserbar dos lokaleedades para esta tardeh/nocheh

In the stalls/in the balcony.
De patio de butacas/de anfiteatro.
deh pat-yo deh bootakas/deh anfeeteh-atro

How much are tickets for the stalls/for the balcony?
¿Cuánto cuesta la entrada de patio de butacas/anfiteatro?
kwanto kwesta la entrada deh pat-yo deh bootakas/anfeeteh-atro

I'll pick them up later on.
Pasaré más tarde a recogerlas.
pasareh mas tardeh a rekoHairlas

I'll meet you in the foyer.
Quedamos en el vestíbulo.
kehdamos en el besteeboolo

CLEANING THINGS

Where's the nearest dry cleaner's?
¿Dónde queda la tintorería más cercana?
dondeh kehda la teentoreree-a mas thairkana

Can you clean this jacket/these trousers for me?
¿Me pueden limpiar esta chaqueta/estos pantalones?
meh pwehden leemp-yar esta chakehta/estos pantalones

When will they be ready?
¿Para cuándo estarán?
para kwando estaran

RESPONSES

Esta tarde.
esta tardeh
This afternoon.

Mañana.
man-yana
Tomorrow.

Pasado mañana.
pasado man-yana
The day after tomorrow.

Do you have some clothes pegs?
¿Tiene pinzas para la ropa?
t-yeneh peenthas para la ropa

Is it ok if I hang my washing out on the roof?
¿Se puede tender la ropa en la terraza del tejado?
seh pwehden tendair la ropa en la terratha del teh-нado

COMMANDS

When speaking to people with the **usted** or **ustedes** forms, you make commands by removing the **-ar**, **-er** or **-ir** from the verb as given in the dictionary section and adding these endings:

	singular	*plural*
hablar (to speak)	**habl-e**	**habl-en**
comer (to eat)	**com-a**	**com-an**
abrir (to open)	**abr-a**	**abr-an**

> **Speak slowly please.**
> Hable despacio, por favor.
> *ableh despath-yo por favor*

When the command is negative (when you are telling someone NOT to do something) you just put **no** in front of the verb using the forms as listed above:

> **Don't speak so fast.**
> ¡No hable tan deprisa!
> *no ableh tan dehpreesa*

> **Don't eat that!**
> ¡No coma eso!
> *no koma eso*

> **Don't open it yet!**
> ¡No lo abra todavía!
> *no lo abra todabee-a*

To give commands to people addressed as **tú** and **vosotros**, remove the endings **-ar**, **-er**, and **-ir** from the verb and add these endings:

	tú	vosotros
hablar (to speak)	**habl-a**	**habl-ad**
comer (to eat)	**com-e**	**com-ed**
abrir (to open)	**abr-e**	**abr-id**

To form a negative command (to tell someone not to do something), **no** is placed in front of the verb and the endings change:

in the singular	in the plural
a – es	ad – éis
e – as	ed – áis
	id – áis

Please speak Spanish, don't speak English. (said to one person)
Por favor, habla español, no hables inglés.
por favor abla espan-yol no ables een-glehs

(said to several people)
Por favor, hablad español, no habléis inglés.
por favor ablad espan-yol no ablays een-glehs

COMPARISONS

To say something is biggER than something else you put the word **más** in front of the adjective (or adverb):

caro – expensive   **más caro** – more expensive

grande – big   **más grande** – bigger

Aren't there any cheaper seats?
¿No hay localidades más baratas?
no i lokaleedades mas baratas

Could you speak more slowly please?
¿Podría hablar más despacio?
podree-a ablar mas despath-yo

To say that something is, for example, the MOST expensive or the biggEST then you put **el más**, **la más**, **los más** or **las más** in front of the adjective (depending on whether the noun is masculine or feminine, singular or plural, see ARTICLES):

Which is the most expensive?
¿Cuál es el más caro?
kwal es el mas karo

The most expensive hotel.
El hotel más caro.
el oh-tel mas karo

The biggest beach.
La playa más grande.
la plïya mas grandeh

Some irregular forms:

bueno	good	**mejor**	*meHor*	better
grande	big	**mayor**	*ma-yor*	bigger
				older
malo	bad	**peor**	*peh-or*	worse
pequeño	small	**menor**	*mehnor*	younger

el mejor	the best
el mayor	the biggest
	the oldest
el peor	the worst
el menor	the youngest

(Of course, **más pequeño** can be said to mean 'smaller').

Some more examples:

My brother is MORE intelligent THAN I am.
Mi hermano es MÁS inteligente QUE yo.
mee airmano es mas eenteleeHenteh keh yo

I'm AS tall AS you (are).
Soy TAN alta COMO tú.
soy tan alta komo too

COMPLAINTS

The ... isn't working.
El/la ... no funciona.
el/la ... no foonth-yona

There's no light in my room.
No hay luz en mi habitación.
no i looth en mee abeetath-yon

There's no toilet paper.
No hay papel higiénico.
no i papel eeн-yeneeko

There's something wrong with this.
Esto no funciona bien.
esto no foonth-yona b-yen

It tastes very peculiar.
Tiene un sabor muy raro.
t-yeneh oon sabor mwee raro

It's still not working properly.
Sigue sin funcionar bien.
seegeh seen foonth-yonar b-yen

I'm not happy about it.
Eso no me parece bien.
eso no meh parehteh b-yen

I want my money back.
Quiero que me devuelvan el dinero.
k-yehro keh meh debwelban el deenehro

I really think you should accept responsibility.
Sinceramente creo que debería usted
responsabilizarse.
seenthairamenteh kreh-o keh debairee-a oostehd
responsabeeleetharseh

CONVERSIONS

inches
1 inch = 2.54 centimetres

metres
1 metre = 39.37 inches or 1.09 yards

kilometres
conversion: kilometres divided by 8, times 5 = miles

kilometres:	1	5	8	10	25	100
miles:	0.6	3.1	5	6.25	15.6	62.5

miles
conversion: miles divided by 5, times 8 = kilometres

miles:	1	3	5	10	20	100
kilometres:	1.6	4.8	8	16	32	160

kilos
conversion: kilos divided by 5, times 11 = pounds

kilos:	1	4	5	10	20	30	40
pounds:	2.2	8.8	11	22	44	66	88

pounds
1 pound = 0.45 kilos
conversion: pounds divided by 11, times 5 = kilos

litres
1 litre = approx. 1.75 pints or 0.22 gallons

Centigrade
conversion: C divided by 5, times 9, plus 32 = F

Centigrade:	10	18	25	28	30	34
Fahrenheit:	50	64	77	82	86	93

conversion: F minus 32, divided by 9, times 5 = C

DANCING AND DISCOS

Let's go to a disco.
¡Vamos a una discoteca!
bamos a oona deeskoteka

Where can we go to dance?
¿Dónde podemos ir a bailar?
dondeh podehmos eer a bilar

Do you want to dance?
¿Quieres bailar?
k-yehres bilar

Fancy another dance?
¿Te apetece bailar otra?
teh apetehteh bilar otra

I can't do that dance.
Yo no sé bailar eso.
yo no seh bilar eso

Are you here by yourself?
¿Estás solo/sola?
estas solo/sola

Great music!
¡Qué buena música!
keh bwena mooseeka

I can't hear you.
No te oigo.
no teh oygo

Let's go to the bar.
¡Vamos al bar!
bamos al bar

DAYS

Monday	**lunes**	*loones*
Tuesday	**martes**	*martes*
Wednesday	**miércoles**	*m-yehrkoles*
Thursday	**jueves**	*Hwehbes*
Friday	**viernes**	*b-yairnes*
Saturday	**sábado**	*sabado*
Sunday	**domingo**	*domeen-go*

On Monday.
El lunes.
el loones

On Tuesday evening.
El martes por la tarde.
el martes por la tardeh

On Saturdays.
Los sábados.
los sabados

On Saturday nights.
Los sábados por la noche.
los sabados por la nocheh

Yesterday.
Ayer.
a-yair

Yesterday morning.
Ayer por la mañana.
a-yair por la man-yana

In the mornings.
Por la mañana.
por la man-yana

In the evenings.
Por la tarde.
por la tardeh

At nights.
Por la noche.
por la nocheh

This afternoon.
Esta tarde.
esta tardeh

The day before yesterday.
Anteayer.
anteh-a-yair

Tomorrow.
Mañana.
man-yana

Tomorrow afternoon.
Mañana por la tarde.
man-yana por la tardeh

The day after tomorrow.
Pasado mañana.
pasado man-yana

Next week.
La semana que viene.
la semana keh bee-eneh

DECLINING, SAYING NO

No thank you.
No, gracias.
no grath-yas

That's very kind, but no thanks.
Muy amable pero no, gracias.
mwee amableh pairo no grath-yas

Thanks all the same though.
Gracias de todas formas.
grath-yas deh todas formas

I don't really want to.
No tengo muchas ganas.
no ten-go moochas ganas

I don't really want one thanks.
De verdad que no (lo) quiero, gracias.
deh bairdad keh no (lo) k-yehro grath-yas

Not for me/us thanks.
Para mí/nosotros no, gracias.
para mee/nosotros no grath-yas

Not right now thanks.
Ahora no, gracias.
a-ora no grath-yas

No no, I'm not interested.
No, no , no me interesa.
no no no meh eenterehsa

I said no!
¡He dicho que no!
eh deecho keh no

DENTIST

I think I need a filling.
Creo que necesito un empaste.
kreh-o keh netheseeto oon empasteh

I've got/he's got a loose tooth.
Se me/le mueve un diente.
seh meh/leh mwehbeh oon d-yenteh

I've got/she's got terrible toothache.
Tengo/tiene un dolor de muelas espantoso.
ten-go/t-yeneh oon dolor deh mwehlas espantoso

Can you give me/him an injection?
¿Me/le puede poner una inyección?
meh/leh pwehdeh ponair oona een-yekth-yon

What will it cost?
¿Cuánto va a costar?
kwanto ba a kostar

Could you write the cost down?
¿Me puede escribir el importe?
meh pwehdeh eskreebeer el eemporteh

Can you pull it out?
¿Me lo puede sacar?
meh lo pwehdeh sakar

> **Abra la boca.**
> *abra la boka*
> Open wide.

> **Hay que sacarlo.**
> *i keh sakarlo*
> It'll have to come out.

> **Esto no va a doler.**
> *esto no ba a dolair*
> This won't hurt.

DIRECTIONS

Can you tell me the way to ...?
¿Me puede decir por dónde se va a ...?
meh pwehdeh detheer por dondeh seh ba a

I'm looking for la Calle de Argensola.
Estoy buscando la Calle de Argensola.
estoy booskando la kiyeh deh arHensola

Which is the best bus for getting to ...?
¿Qué autobús viene mejor para ir a ...?
keh owtoboos b-yeneh meHor para eer a

Could you point it out on the map/street map?
¿Me lo puede indicar en el mapa/plano?
meh lo pwehdeh eendeekar en el mapa/plano

Which road is it to ..?
¿Cuál es la carretera de ...?
kwal es la karretaira deh

Excuse me, which street is this?
Por favor, ¿qué calle es ésta?
por favor keh kiyeh es esta

How do I get there?
¿Cómo voy hasta allí?
komo boy asta a-yee

Is it walkable?
¿Se puede ir andando?
seh pwehdeh eer andando

Could you just point out the general direction?
¿Podría indicarme más o menos hacia dónde está?
podree-a eendeekarmeh mas o mehnos athee-a dondeh esta

RESPONSES

Coja la primera a la derecha.
koна la preemaira a la derecha
Take the first right.

Coja la segunda a la izquierda.
koна la segoonda a la eethk-yairda
Take the second left.

Llegando al primer semáforo, a la izquierda.
yehgando al preemair semaforo a la eethk-yairda
Left at the first set of traffic lights.

Siga todo recto.
seega todo rekto
Go straight on.

Deje atrás el siguiente semáforo.
deнeh atras el seeg-yenteh semaforo
Go straight through the next lights.

Al llegar a la iglesia/al banco/al museo, tuerza a la derecha.
al yehgar a la eeglehs-ya/al banko/al mooseh-o twairtha a la derecha
Go right at the church/bank/museum.

Pase por el puente.
paseh por el pwenteh
Go across the bridge.

Dé la vuelta y siga hasta que ...
day la bwelta ee seega asta keh
Go back this way until ...

Lo siento, yo tampoco soy de aquí.
lo s-yento yo tampoko soy deh akee
Sorry, I'm a stranger here myself.

DISAGREEING WITH PEOPLE

No, that's not right.
No, eso no está bien.
no eso no esta b-yen

I don't think so.
Creo que no.
kreh-o keh no

Oh no.
Ah, no.
a no

I think you're wrong.
Creo que te equivocas/se equivoca.
kreh-o keh teh ekeebokas/seh ekeeboka

He's wrong.
Está equivocado.
esta ekeebokado

They're wrong.
Están equivocados.
estan ekeebokados

I don't agree with that.
No estoy de acuerdo.
no estoy deh akwairdo

Definitely not.
Rotundamente no.
rotoondamenteh no

No way!
¡Ni hablar!
nee ablar

Nonsense!
¡Qué va!
keh ba

DISLIKES

I don't like beer/this hotel.
No me gusta la cerveza/este hotel.
no meh goosta la thairbehtha/esteh otel

I don't like olives.
No me gustan las aceitunas.
no meh goostan las athaytoonas

I don't like swimming/sunbathing.
No me gusta nadar/tomar el sol.
no meh goosta nadar/tomar el sol

I don't like it.
No me gusta.
no meh goosta

She doesn't like Miguel.
No le cae bien Miguel.
no leh ka-eh b-yen meegel

I can't stand ....
No soporto ....
no soporto

It doesn't taste very nice.
No está nada bueno.
no esta nada bweno

That's awful!
¡Qué horror!
keh orror

It was terrible.
Fue horrible.
fweh orreebleh

DOCTOR

Can you call a doctor?
¿Puede llamar a un médico?
pwehdeh yamar a oon medeeko

I'm a doctor/a nurse.
Soy médico/enfermera.
soy medeeko/enfermaira

He's had an accident.
Ha tenido un accidente.
a teneedo oon aktheedenteh

I'm/he's/she's ill.
Estoy/está enfermo/a.
estoy/esta enfairmo/a

It's my stomach.
Es el estómago.
es el estomago

It's my back.
Es la espalda.
es la espalda

It's my chest.
Es el pecho.
es el pecho

He/she fell over.
Se cayó.
seh kiyo

I think it's broken.
Me parece que está roto.
meh parehtheh keh esta roto

He's/she's unconscious.
Ha perdido el conocimiento.
a pairdeedo el konotheem-yento

44

It hurts here.
Me duele aquí.
meh dwehleh akee

It's a very sharp pain.
Es un dolor muy agudo.
es oon dolor mwee agoodo

I've got insurance.
Tengo seguro.
ten-go segooro

What will it cost?
¿Cuánto costará?
kwanto kostara

RESPONSES

No es nada grave.
no es nada grabeh
It's nothing serious.

Va a tener que ir al hospital.
ba a tenair keh eer al ospeetal
You'll/he'll/she'll have to go in to hospital.

Va a tener que operarse.
ba a tenair keh operarseh
You'll/he'll/she'll need an operation.

Está roto.
esta roto
It's broken.

Es un infarto.
es oon eenfarto
It's a heart attack.

Es una intoxicación alimentaria.
es oona eentoxeekath-yon aleementar-ya
It's food poisoning.

Vaya con esto a una farmacia.
biya kon esto a oona farmath-ya
Take this to a chemist.

DRINKS

What are you drinking?
¿Qué bebes/bebe?
keh bebes/bebeh

A coffee/tea please.
Un café/té, por favor.
oon kafeh/teh por favor

Two coffees and a beer.
Dos cafés y una cerveza.
dos kafehs ee oona thairbehtha

Two white wines please.
Dos (vinos) blancos, por favor
dos (beenos) blankos por favor

A bottle of red wine.
Una botella de vino tinto.
oona boteh-ya deh beeno teento

Dry wine/sweet wine/medium dry wine.
Vino seco/vino dulce/vino semi-seco.
beeno seko/beeno dooltheh/beeno semee-seko

The same again please.
Lo mismo, por favor.
lo meezmo por favor

No ice for me thanks.
No me ponga hielo, por favor.
no meh pon-ga yehlo por favor

I'd rather have draught beer.
Prefiero tomar una caña.
pref-yehro tomar oona kan-ya

It's my/your round.
Esta ronda me toca a mí/te toca a tí.
esta ronda meh toka a mee/teh toka a tee

DRINKS LIST

el agua mineral *agwa meenairal* mineral water
el anís *anees* aniseed-flavoured drink
el batido *bateedo* milkshake
las bebidas alcohólicas *bebeedas alkoleekas* alcoholic drinks
las bebidas refrescantes *bebeedas refreskantes* soft drinks
el café con leche *kafeh kon lecheh* white coffee
el café solo *kafeh solo* black coffee
la caña *kan-ya* glass of draught beer
la cerveza *thairbehza* beer
el champán *champan* champagne
la clara *klara* shandy
con gas *kon gas* fizzy, sparkling
el coñac *kon-yak* brandy
la gaseosa *gaseh-osa* lemonade
la ginebra *Heenehbra* gin
el granizado *graneethado* crushed ice drink
la horchata (de chufa) *orchata (deh choofa)* tigernut milk
la infusión *eenfoos-yon* herb tea
el jerez *Haireth* sherry
el jugo de ... *Hoogo deh ... ...* juice
la leche *lecheh* milk
la leche merengada *lecheh mairengada* iced milk with meringue and cinnamon
la manzanilla *manthanee-ya* camomile tea
el mosto *mosto* grape juice
la sangría *sangree-a* mixture of red wine, lemonade, spirits and fruit
la sidra *seedra* cider
sin gas *seen gas* still
la tila *teela* lime tea
el vino del país *beeno del pa-ees* local wine
el vino de mesa *beeno deh mehsa* table wine
el vino rosado *beeno rosado* rosé wine
la vodka con naranja/piña *bodka kon naranHa/peen-ya* vodka and orange/pineapple
el zumo *thoomo* fruit juice
el zumo de limón *thoomo deh leemon* lemon juice
el zumo de naranja *thoomo deh naran-Ha* orange juice

DRIVING

(see also CAR ACCIDENTS, GARAGE, RENTALS)

Can I park here?
¿Puedo aparcar aquí?
pwehdo aparkar akee

Where can I park the car?
¿Dónde puedo aparcar el coche?
dondeh pwehdo aparkar el kocheh

Where is the nearest petrol station?
¿Dónde queda la gasolinera más cercana?
dondeh kehda la gasoleenaira mas thairkana

Is this the road for …?
¿Es ésta la carretera de …?
es esta la karretaira deh

We came by car.
Vinimos en coche.
beeneemos en kocheh

We're going to drive to …
Nos vamos a … en el coche.
nos bamos a … en el kocheh

How long does it take to drive there?
¿Cuánto se tarda en coche?
kwanto seh tarda en kocheh

It's in the car.
Está en el coche.
esta en el kocheh

Let's take my car.
¡Vamos en mi coche!
bamos en mee kocheh

EMERGENCIES

(see also *THEFT*)

I'm lost.
Me he perdido.
meh eh pairdeedo

It's broken.
Se ha roto.
seh a roto

The coin's stuck.
La moneda se ha quedado atascada.
la monehda seh a kehdado ataskada

It's stuck. (door etc)
Se ha encajado.
seh a enkaнado

Help!
¡Socorro!
sokorro

Call the police!
¡Llamen a la policía!
yamen a la poleethee-a

There's a fire!
¡Hay un incendio!
i oon eenthend-yo

The tap won't turn off.
El grifo no se puede cerrar.
el greefo no seh pwehdeh thairrar

There's a smell of gas.
Huele a gas.
wehleh a gas

The toilet won't flush.
La cisterna del váter no funciona.
la theestairna del batair no foonth-yona

The . . . gives you an electric shock.
El/la . . . da calambre.
el/la . . . da kalambreh

Get a doctor!
¡Llamen a un médico!
yamen a oon medeeko

He's had an accident.
Ha tenido un accidente.
a teneedo oon aktheedenteh

It's very urgent.
Es muy urgente.
es mwee oorHenteh

I've locked myself out.
Me he dejado la llave dentro y no puedo entrar.
meh eh deHado la yabeh dentro ee no pwehdo entrar

This man is pestering me.
Este hombre me está molestando.
esteh ombreh meh esta molestando

Does anyone speak English?
¿Alguien habla inglés?
alg-yen abla een-gles

EXPLAINING THINGS

(see also INTENTIONS)

It's necessary to ...
Hay que ...
i keh

You have to push this button.
Tienes/tiene que pulsar este botón.
t-yenes/t-yeneh keh poolsar esteh boton

It's because of the ...
Es debido al/a la ...
es debeedo al/a la

You need ...
Necesitas/necesita ...
netheseetas/netheseeta

I didn't know that.
No lo sabía.
no lo sabee-a

It wasn't possible to ...
No fue posible ...
no fweh poseebleh

She didn't understand you, that's why.
Eso es sencillamente que no te/le entendió.
eso es senthee-yamenteh keh no teh/leh entend-yo

If you ... then ...
Si tú/usted ... entonces ...
see too/ostehd ... entonthes

I'll get an interpreter.
Voy a buscar un intérprete.
boy a booskar oon eentairpreteh

FEEL: HOW YOU FEEL

I'm/he's hungry.
Tengo/tiene hambre.
ten-go/t-yeneh ambreh

I'm/we're thirsty.
Tengo/tenemos sed.
ten-go/tenehmos sed

I'm tired/she's tired.
Estoy cansado/está cansada.
estoy kansado/esta kansada

I'm/he's bored.
Estoy/está aburrido.
estoy/esta aboorreedo

I'm/they're sleepy.
Tengo/tienen sueño.
ten-go/t-yenen swehn-yo

I feel fine thanks.
Me encuentro bien, gracias.
meh enkwentro b-yen grath-yas

I feel great!
¡Me encuentro estupendamente!
meh enkwentro estoopendamenteh

I feel much better.
Me encuentro mucho mejor.
meh enkwentro moocho meHor

He's much better thanks.
Está mucho mejor, gracias.
esta moocho meHor grath-yas

How are you feeling?
¿Cómo te encuentras/se encuentra?
komo teh enkwentras/seh enkwentra

FLYING

Can you take us to the airport?
¿Nos puede llevar al aeropuerto?
nos pwehdeh yehbar al iropwairto

Where does the airport bus stop?
¿Dónde para el autobús del aeropuerto?
dondeh para el owtoboos del iropwairto

Is this ok for the airport?
¿Lleva éste al aeropuerto?
yehba esteh al iropwairto

I'd like a single/return ticket to ...
Quería un billete de ida/ida y vuelta a ...
kehree-a oon beeyehteh deh eeda/eeda ee bwelta a

Non-smoking please.
No fumadores, por favor.
no foomadores por favor

Smoking please.
Fumadores, por favor.
foomadores por favor

A window seat if possible.
Asiento de ventanilla a ser posible.
as-yento deh bentaneeya a ser poseebleh

Which gate is it?
¿Qué puerta es?
keh pwairta es

What time is the next flight?
¿A qué hora es el próximo vuelo?
a keh ora es el proxeemo bwehlo

FORBIDDING

You mustn't ...
No tienes/tiene que ...
no t-yenes/t-yeneh keh

You shouldn't do that.
No debes/debe hacer eso.
no dehbes/deh-beh athair eso

Don't do that.
No hagas/haga eso.
no agas/a-ga eso

Don't do anything until I say so.
No hagas/haga nada hasta que yo diga.
no agas/a-ga nada asta keh yo deega

He's not to smoke.
Que no fume.
keh no foomeh

That's not allowed.
Eso no está permitido.
eso no esta pairmeeteedo

Stop that right now!
¡Basta ya!
basta ya

No way!
¡Ni hablar!
nee ablar

> Se ruega no ...
> *seh rwehga no*
> Please do not ...

FUTURE

To talk about what is going to happen in the future you can very often use the present tense (see *PRESENT*). English works in a similar way, for example:

Our train leaves at 11.00 tomorrow.
Nuestro tren sale mañana a los once.
nwestro tren saleh man-yana a las ontheh

I'm going home next week.
Vuelvo a casa la semana que viene.
bwelbo a kasa la semana keh b-yeneh

Spanish often uses the present tense where English uses the future:

I'll be right back.
Vuelvo en seguida.
bwelbo en segeeda

The actual future tense in Spanish (I will, you will etc) is formed by adding the following endings to the infinitive form of the verb (as given in the dictionary section). The same endings are used for verbs ending in **-ar**, **-er** and **-ir**.

hablar-é	*ablar-eh*	I will speak
hablar-ás	*ablar-as*	you will speak
hablar-á	*ablar-a*	he/she/you will speak
hablar-emos	*ablarehmos*	we will speak
hablar-éis	*ablar-ays*	you will speak
hablar-án	*ablaran*	they/you will speak

There are several irregular futures:

decir – diré
I will say

hacer – haré
I will do

poder – podré
I will be able

poner – pondré
I will put

querer – querré
I will want

saber – sabré
I will know

salir – saldré
I will leave

tener – tendré
I will have

venir – vendré
I will come

To express the immediate future you can also use **IR + A** + INFINITIVE:

Voy a salir.
boy a saleer
I'm going to go out.

Vamos a visitar a mi tía.
bamos a beeseetar a mee tee-a
We're going to visit my aunt.

GARAGES

(see also DRIVING)

30 litres of this type please.
30 litros de esta clase, por favor.
traynta leetros deh esta klaseh por favor

Could you fill it up?
Lleno, por favor.
yehno por favor

1 litre of oil.
1 litro de aceite.
oon leetro deh athayteh

Do you do repairs?
¿Hacen reparaciones?
athen reparath-yones

Could you have a look at the front brakes/rear brakes?
¿Podría revisar los frenos delanteros/traseros?
podreea rehbeesar los frehnos dehlantairos/trasairos

I think there's something wrong with the clutch.
Me parece que el embrague no funciona bien.
meh parehtheh keh el embrageh no foonth-yona b-yen

It's losing water.
Pierde agua.
p-yehrdeh agwa

It's overheating.
Se calienta.
seh kal-yenta

It keeps cutting out.
El motor se para.
el motor seh para

It takes a long time to start.
Tarda mucho en arrancar.
tarda moocho en arrankar

The steering is very slack.
La dirección anda muy floja.
la deerekth-yon anda mwee floнa

The door won't lock.
La puerta no cierra.
la pwairta no th-yehra

The lights are faulty.
Las luces fallan.
las loothes fiyan

I need a new indicator bulb.
Necesito una bombilla nueva para el intermitente.
netheseeto oona bombeeya nwehba para el eentermeetenteh

Can you do it now?
¿Lo puede hacer ahora?
lo pwehdeh athair a-ora

Can you do it today?
¿Lo tendrá para hoy?
lo tendra para oy

When can I pick it up?
¿Cuando puedo pasar a recogerlo?
kwando pwehdo pasar a rekoнairlo

HAIRDRESSER

Just a trim please.
Igualarme nada más, por favor.
eegwalarmeh nada mas por favor

Could you take about 5 centimetres off all round?
¿Me corta unos cinco centímetros todo por igual?
meh korta oonos theenko thenteemetros todo por eegwal

Could you tidy up the ends?
¿Me recorta las puntas?
meh rekorta las poontas

Not too short.
No demasiado corto.
no dehmas-yado korto

I'd like it layered.
Lo quiero a capas.
lo k-yehro a kapas

On top.
Arriba.
arreeba

At the sides.
A los lados.
a los lados

I'd like it a lot shorter.
Lo quiero mucho más corto.
lo k-yehro moocho mas korto

Up to about here.
Más o menos hasta aquí.
mas o mehnos asta akee

Just over the ears.
Tapando un poco la oreja.
tapando oon poko la oreнa

A shampoo and set please.
Lavado y marcado, por favor.
labado ee markado por favor

Can you put highlights in?
¿Me pone mechas?
meh poneh mechas

Can you get rid of the grey hairs?
¿Me puede teñir las canas?
meh pwehdeh ten-yeer las kanas

Can you do the roots?
¿Me tiñe las raíces?
meh teen-yeh las ra-eethes

Can you give me a perm?
¿Me puede hacer una permanente?
meh pwehdeh athair oona pairmanenteh

Curly hair/straight hair.
Pelo rizado/pelo liso.
pehlo reethado/pehlo leeso

RESPONSES

¿Le pongo suavizante?
leh pon-go swabeethanteh
Would you like conditioner?

¿Secado a mano?
sekado a mano
A blow dry?

HELLO – GOODBYE

Hello.
¡Hola!
ola

Hi there.
¿Qué hay?
keh i

Goodbye.
Adiós.
ad-yos

Cheerio.
Hasta la vista.
asta la beesta

See you later.
Hasta luego.
asta lwehgo

Good morning/good afternoon.
Buenos días/buenas tardes.
bwenos deeas/bwenas tardes

Good evening.
(early) Buenas tardes; (late) Buenas noches.
bwenas tardes, bwenas noches

Good night.
Buenas noches.
bwenas noches

Pleased to meet you.
Mucho gusto.
moocho goosto

It was nice meeting you.
Encantado de conocerle.
enkantado deh konothairleh

HITCH-HIKING

Are you going to ...?
¿Va a ...?
ba a

Are you going anywhere near ...?
¿Va en dirección a ...?
ba en deerekth-yon a

Can you give me/us a lift?
¿Me/nos puede llevar?
meh/nos pwehdeh yehbar

We've been standing here for two hours.
Hemos estado aquí plantados dos horas.
ehmos estado akee plantados dos oras

Do you have room for the four of us?
¿Cabemos los cuatro?
kabehmos los kwatro

Can you drop us off here/at the next services?
¿Nos puede dejar aquí/en la próxima zona de servicios?
nos pwehdeh deнar akee/en la proxeema thona deh sairbeeth-yos

That's very kind of you.
Muy amable.
mwee amableh

RESPONSES

¿A dónde va?
a dondeh ba
Where are you going?

No voy más que hasta ...
no boy mas keh asta
I'm only going as far as ...

63

HOSPITAL

(*see also DOCTOR*)

Can you take us to the hospital?
¿Nos puede llevar al hospital?
nos pwehdeh yehbar al ospeetal

To the casualty department.
A urgencias.
a oorHenth-yas

To the maternity unit.
A maternidad.
a matairneedad

Which ward is he/she in?
¿En qué sala está?
en keh sala esta

How is he/she doing?
¿Qué tal sigue?
keh tal seegeh

RESPONSES

Mejor/regular.
meHor/regoolar
Better/satisfactory.

When are visiting hours?
¿Cuáles son las horas de visita?
kwales son las oras deh beeseeta

How long will I/he have to stay in for?
¿Cuánto tiempo tendré/tendrá que estar hospitalizado?
kwanto t-yempo tendreh/tendra keh estar ospeetaleethado

Is treatment covered by this insurance?
Este seguro ¿cubre la asistencia médica?
esteh segooro koobreh la aseestenth-ya medeeka

HOTELS

(see also ROOMS, SELF-CATERING)

Do you have a room for one night?
¿Tiene habitación para una noche?
t-yeneh abeetath-yon para oona nocheh

For two nights/for a week.
Para dos noches/para una semana.
para dos noches/para oona semana

Do you have a room for one person?
¿Tiene habitación para una persona?
t-yeneh abeetath-yon para oona pairsona

A single room/a double room.
Una habitación individual/una habitación doble.
*oona abeetath-yon eendeebeedoo-al/oona abeetath-yon
   dobleh*

For two people/for two adults and one child.
Para dos personas/para dos y un niño
para dos pairsonas/para dos ee oon neen-yo

I have a reservation.
He hecho una reserva.
eh ehcho oona resairba

How much is it per night?
¿Cuál es el precio por noche?
kwal es el preth-yo por nocheh

Could you write the cost down?
¿Puede darme el importe por escrito?
pwehdeh darmeh el eemporteh por eskreeto

We'd like a room with two single beds.
Querríamos una habitación de dos camas.
kehrree-amos oona abeetath-yon deh dos kamas

We'd like a room with a double bed.
Querríamos una habitación con cama de matrimonio.
kehrree-amos oona abeetath-yon kon kama deh matreemon-yo

Can we see the room?
¿Podemos ver la habitación?
podehmos bair la abeetath-yon

RESPONSES

¿Su nombre, por favor?
soo nombreh por favor
Your name please?

¿Me firma aquí?
meh feerma akee
Could you sign here?

¿Me permite el pasaporte?
meh pairmeeteh el pasaporteh
Can I see your passport?

¿Cómo desea pagar?
komo deseh-a pagar
How will you be paying?

By credit card/cash.
Con tarjeta de crédito/en efectivo.
kon tarHehta deh krehdeeto/en efekteebo

Can I have the bill for room 12 please.
La cuenta de la habitación doce, por favor.
la kwenta deh la abeetath-yon dotheh por favor

I'd like to stay another night.
Querría quedarme una noche más.
kehrree-a kehdarmeh oona nocheh mas

IDIOMS

Está lloviendo a mares.
esta yob-yendo a mares
It's raining cats and dogs.

Está más borracho que una cuba.
esta mas borracho keh oona kooba
He's as drunk as a newt.

No pegamos ojo en toda la noche.
no pegamos oнo en toda la nocheh
We didn't sleep a wink all night.

He dormido como un lirón.
eh dormeedo komo oon leeron
I slept like a log.

Cuesta un dineral.
kwesta oon deenairal
It costs a fortune.

Estoy sin blanca.
estoy seen blanka
I'm broke.

Está usted más loco que una cabra.
esta ostehd mas loko keh oona kabra
You're as mad as a hatter.

Te está tomando el pelo.
teh esta tomando el pehlo
He's pulling your leg.

No tiene un pelo de tonto.
no t-yeneh oon pehlo deh tonto
He's no fool.

Lo pasamos bomba.
lo pasamos bomba
We had a great time.

INTENTIONS

What are you going to do?
¿Qué vas/va a hacer?
keh bas/ba a athair

I'll be back soon.
No tardaré en volver.
no tardareh en bolbair

I'll bring it back this afternoon/tomorrow.
Lo traeré esta tarde/mañana.
lo tra-ereh esta tardeh/man-yana

I'll go to the bank and then come back with the money.
Iré al banco y luego volveré con el dinero.
eereh al banko ee lwehgo bolbaireh kon el deenehro

I'll give it to him for you.
Se lo daré de tu/su parte.
seh lo dareh deh too/soo parteh

I'll leave this here as a deposit.
Dejo esto de señal.
deHo esto deh sen-yal

I'm coming back next week.
Vuelvo la semana que viene.
bwelbo la semana keh b-yeneh

I'll do something about it, I promise.
Me ocuparé del asunto, te/se lo prometo.
meh okopareh del asoonto teh/seh lo promehto

I'll go and get ...
Voy a por ...
boy a por

INVITING PEOPLE

Would you like to ...?
¿Quieres/quiere ...?
k-yehres/k-yehreh

Would you like to come with us?
¿Quieres/quiere venir con nosotros?
k-yehres/k-yehreh beneer kon nosotros

Would you like to have a drink?
¿Quieres/quiere beber algo?
k-yehres/k-yehreh bebair algo

Would you like to come out this evening?
¿Te/le apetece salir esta tarde?
teh/leh apetehtheh saleer esta tardeh

What are you doing tonight?
¿Qué haces/hace esta noche?
keh athes/a-theh esta nocheh

How about going out for a meal this evening?
¿Y si saliéramos a cenar esta noche?
ee see sal-yehramos a thehnar esta nocheh

We'd like to invite you out.
Queremos invitarte/invitarle a salir.
kerehmos eenbeetarteh/eenbeetarleh a saleer

Thanks for the invitation, but ...
Gracias por la invitación pero ...
grath-yas por la eenbeetath-yon pairo

LIKES

I like this wine.
Me gusta este vino.
meh goosta esteh beeno

I like olives a lot.
Me gustan mucho las aceitunas.
meh goostan moocho las athaytoonas

I like swimming/sunbathing.
Me gusta nadar/tomar el sol.
meh goosta nadar/tomar el sol

She/he likes him/her.
Le cae bien.
leh ka-eh b-yen

I like it.
Me gusta.
meh goosta

I like it here.
Me gusta esto.
meh goosta esto

I love you.
Te quiero.
teh k-yehro

I love the wine/these colours.
Me encanta el vino/me encantan estos colores.
me enkanta el beeno/meh enkantan estos kolores

It was fantastic.
Fue maravilloso.
fweh marabeeyoso

MAP

MENU READER

aceitunas negras *athaytoonas nehgras* black olives
aceitunas verdes *athaytoonas bairdes* green olives
acelgas *athelgas* kind of spinach
aguacate *agwakateh* avocado
albóndigas *albondeegas* meatballs
alcachofas con jamón *alkachofas kon Hamon* artichokes with ham
alcachofas salteadas *alkachofas salteh-adas* sautéed artichokes
almejas a la marinera *almeHas a la mareenaira* clams stewed in wine and parsley
alubias con ... *aloob-yas kon* beans with ...
anchoas *ancho-as* anchovies
angulas *an-goolas* baby eels
apio *ap-yo* celery
arenque *arenkeh* herring
arroz a la cubana *arroth a la koobana* boiled rice with fried eggs and bananas
arroz blanco *arroth blanko* boiled (white) rice
arroz con leche *arroth kon lecheh* rice pudding
asados *asados* roast meats
atún al horno *atoon al orno* baked tuna

bacalao al pil pil *bakalao al peel peel* cod with chilis and garlic
batido de chocolate *bateedo deh chokolateh* chocolate milkshake
batido de fresa *bateedo deh frehsa* strawberry milkshake
batido de frutas *bateedo deh frootas* fruit milkshake
batido de plátano *bateedo deh platano* banana milkshake
batido de vainilla *bateedo deh bineeya* vanilla milkshake
berenjenas fritas *berenHehnas freetas* fried aubergines
besugo al horno *besoogo al orno* baked sea bream
bistec de ternera *beestek deh ternaira* veal steak
bizcocho *beethkocho* sponge
bizcochos *beethkochos* sponge fingers
bonito al horno *boneeto al orno* baked tuna
bonito con tomate *boneeto kon tomateh* tuna with tomato sauce
boquerones fritos *bokairones freetos* fried (fresh) anchovies
brazo de gitano *bratho deh Heetano* type of Swiss roll
buñuelos *boon-yoowehlos* light fried pastries
buñuelos de bacalao *boon-yoowehlos deh bakalao* dried salted

cod mixed with batter and then fried

cabrito asado *kabreeto asado* roast kid

calamares a la romana *kalamares a la romana* squid rings fried in batter

calamares en su tinta *kalamares en soo teenta* squid cooked in their own ink

calamares fritos *kalamares freetos* fried squid rings

caldo de ... *kaldo deh* clear ... soup

caldo gallego *kaldo ga-yehgo* clear soup with green vegetables, beans and pork

callos a la madrileña *ka-yos a la madreelehn-ya* tripe cooked with chilis

camarones *kamarones* baby prawns

canelones *kanelones* canneloni

cangrejos de río *kangreHos deh ree-o* river crabs

carnes *karnes* meats

castañas *kastan-yas* chestnuts

centollo *thento-yo* spider crab

champiñones al ajillo *champeen-yones al a-Heeyo* mushrooms fried with garlic

champiñones a la plancha *champeen-yones a la plancha* grilled mushrooms

chipirones en su tinta *cheepeerones en soo teenta* baby squid cooked in their own ink

chipirones rellenos *cheepeerones reyehnos* stuffed baby squid

chorizo *choreetho* cured red sausage

chuleta de cerdo *choolehta deh thairdo* pork chop

chuleta de cerdo empanada *choolehta deh thairdo empanada* breaded pork chop

chuletas de cordero (con ali-oli) *choolehtas deh kordairo (kon alee-olee)* lamb chops (with garlic mayonnaise)

chuletas de ternera *choolehtas deh ternaira* veal chops

chuletas de ternera empanada *choolehtas deh ternaira empanada* breaded veal chops

chuletón *choolehton* large chop

churros *choorros* fried pastry cut into lengths

cigalas a la parrilla *theegalas a la parreeya* grilled crayfish

cóctel de gambas *koktel deh gambas* prawn cocktail

cóctel de langostinos *koktel deh langosteenos* king prawn cocktail

cóctel de mariscos *koktel deh mareeskos* seafood cocktail

cochinillo asado *kocheeneeyo asado* roast sucking pig

cocido castellano/madrileño *kotheedo kasteh-yano/madreelehn-yo* noodle soup followed by stew made with meat, chickpeas, vegetables, cured red sausage

codornices estofadas *kodorneethes estofadas* stewed quail

coles de bruselas salteadas *koles deh broosehlas salteh-adas* sautéed Brussels sprouts

coliflor *kolee;flor* cauliflower

corejo estofado *koneHo estofado* stewed rabbit

consomé al jerez *konsomeh al Hereth* consommé with sherry

consomé con yema *konsomeh kon yehma* consommé with egg yolk

consomé de ave *konsomeh deh abeh* chicken consommé

copa helada *kopa ehlada* ice cream sundae

cordero asado *kordairo asado* roast lamb

cordero chilindrón *kordairo cheeleendron* lamb stew with onion, tomato and peppers

costillas de cerdo *kosteeyas deh thairdo* pork ribs

crema de cangrejos *krehma deh kangreHos* cream of crab soup

crema de espárragos *krehma deh esparragos* cream of asparagus soup

crema de legumbres *krehma deh legoombres* cream of vegetable soup

crocante *krokanteh* ice cream with chopped nuts

croquetas de jamón *kroketas deh Hamon* ham croquettes

croquetas de pescado *kroketas deh peskado* fish croquettes

cuajada *kwaHada* junket

dulce de membrillo *dooltheh deh membreeyo* quince jelly

empanada gallega *empanada ga-yehga* pie with chicken, cured red sausage, peppers and ham

empanadillas de bonito *empanadeeyas deh boneeto* small tuna pies

empanadillas de carne *empanadeeyas deh karneh* small meat pies

ensalada de lechuga *ensalada deh lechooga* lettuce salad

ensalada de tomate *ensalada deh tomateh* tomato salad

ensalada mixta *ensalada meexta* mixed salad

ensaladilla rusa *ensaladeeya roosa* Russian salad

entrecot a la parrilla *entre-kot a la parreeya* grilled entrecôte

entremeses variados *entrehmeses bar-yados* hors d'oeuvres

escalope a la milanesa *eskalopeh a la meelanehsa* breaded veal with cheese

escalope empanado *eskalopeh empanado* breaded escalope of veal

escarola *eskarola* endive

espaguetis (italiana) *espagetees (eetal-yana)* spaghetti

espárragos *esparragos* asparagus

espinacas a la crema *espeenakas a la krehma* creamed spinach

estofado de liebre *estofado deh lee-ebreh* hare stew

fabada asturiana *fabada astoor-yana* bean stew with red sausage, black pudding and pork

fideos *fideh-os* noodles, vermicelli

filete a la parrilla/a la plancha *feelehteh a la parreeya/a la plancha* grilled (beef) steak

filete de cerdo *feelehteh deh thairdo* pork steak

filete de ternera *feelehteh deh ternaira* veal steak

flan *flan* crème caramel

fresas con nata *frehsas kon nata* strawberries and cream

fruta variada *froota bar-yada* assorted fresh fruit

gambas al ajillo *gambas al a-Heeyo* prawns with garlic

gambas a la plancha *gambas a la plancha* grilled prawns

garbanzos *garbanthos* chickpeas

gazpacho andaluz *gathpacho andalooth* cold soup made with tomatoes, onions, peppers, cucumber, breadcrumbs and garlic

gazpacho manchego *gathpacho manchehgo* rabbit stew with tomato and garlic (sometimes also with partridge)

guisantes salteados con jamón *geesantes salteh-ados kon Hamon* sautéed peas with ham

helado de chocolate *ehlado deh chokolateh* chocolate ice cream

helado de fresa *ehlado deh frehsa* strawberry ice cream

helado de vainilla/mantecado *ehlado deh bineeya/mantekado* vanilla ice cream

hígado encebollado *eegado enthebo-yado* liver in an onion sauce

huevos *wehbos* eggs

huevos a la flamenca *wehbos a la flamenka* baked eggs with sausage, tomato, peas, asparagus and peppers

huevos cocidos/duros *wehbos kotheedos/dooros* hard-boiled eggs

huevos con jamón *wehbos kon Hamon* ham and eggs

huevos con patatas fritas *wehbos kon patatas freetas* fried eggs and chips

huevos fritos *wehbos freetos* fried eggs

huevos fritos con chorizo/jamón *wehbos freetos kon choreetho/Hamon* fried eggs with cured red sausage/ham

huevos pasados por agua *wehbos pasados por agwa* soft-boiled eggs

huevos rellenos *wehbos reh-yehnos* stuffed eggs

huevos revueltos con tomate *wehbos rebweltos kon tomateh* scrambled eggs with tomato

incluye pan, postre y vino *eenkloouyeh pan postreh ee beeno* includes bread, dessert and wine

infusiones *eenfoos-yones* herb teas

jamón (serrano) *Hamon (serrano)* cured ham

jamón de York *Hamon deh york* ham

judías verdes (con jamón) *Hoodeeas bairdes (kon Hamon)* French beans (with ham)

langosta *langosta* lobster

langostinos a la plancha *langosteenos a la plancha* grilled king prawns

leche frita *lecheh freeta* slices of thick custard fried in breadcrumbs

leche merengada *lecheh merengada* milk and meringue sorbet

lengua *leng-wa* tongue

lenguado frito *lengwado freeto* fried sole

lombarda *lombarda* red cabbage

lubina al horno *loobeena al orno* baked sea bass

macarrones *makarrones* macaroni

macarrones gratinados *makarrones grateenados* macaroni cheese

macedonia de frutas *mathedon-ya deh frootas* fruit salad

mantecadas *mantehkadas* small sponge cakes

mantequilla *mantehkeeya* butter

manzanas asadas *manthanas asadas* baked apples

mariscada *mareeskada* cold mixed shellfish

mazapán *mathapan* marzipan
mayonesa *mi-onehsa* mayonnaise
mejillones *meh-Heeyones* mussels
melocotón en almíbar *melokoton en almeebar* tinned peaches
melocotones *melokotones* peaches
melón con jamón *melon kon Hamon* melon with cured ham
menestra de verduras *menestra deh bairdooras* vegetable stew
menú de la casa *menoo deh la kasa* fixed price menu
menú del día *menoo del dee-a* set menu
merluza a la cazuela *mairlootha a la kathwehla* hake casserole
merluza a la romana *mairlootha a la romana* hake steaks in
  batter
merluza frita *mairlootha freeta* fried hake
mermelada *mermelada* jam
mermelada de albaricoque *mermelada deh albareekokeh*
  apricot jam
mermelada de ciruela *mermelada deh theerwehla* plum jam
mermelada de melocotón *mermelada deh melokoton* peach
  jam
mermelada de naranja *mermelada deh naranHa* marmalade
mero a la parrilla *mairo a la parreeya* grilled grouper
mero en salsa verde *mairo en salsa bairdeh* grouper with
  garlic and parsley sauce
mollejas de ternera fritas *mo-yeHas deh ternaira freetas* fried
  sweetbreads
morcilla *mortheeya* black pudding

natillas *nateeyas* cold custard with cinnamon

paella (valenciana) *pa-ehya (balenth-yana)* fried rice with
  various shellfish and chicken
paella de pescado *pa-ehya deh mareesko* fried rice with
  seafood
panaché de verduras *panacheh deh bairdooras* vegetable stew
parrillada de mariscos *parreeyada deh mareeskos* mixed
  grilled shellfish
pasteles *pasteles* cakes
patatas bravas *patatas brabas* potatoes in cayenne sauce
patatas fritas *patatas freetas* chips; crisps
pato a la naranja *pato a la naran-Ha* duck à l'orange
pavo relleno *pabo re-yehno* stuffed turkey
pechuga de pollo *pechooga deh po-yo* chicken breast

pepinillos *pepeeneeyos* gherkins
pepino *pepeeno* cucumber
perdices escabechadas *pairdeethes eskabechadas* marinated partridges
perdices estofadas *pairdeethes estofadas* stewed partridges
perejil *pereHeel* parsley
pescaditos fritos *peem-yentos freetos* fried sprats
pestiños (con miel) *pesteen-yos (kon mee-el)* fried sugared pastries with anis (and honey)
pimientos fritos *peem-yentos freetos* fried peppers
pimientos rellenos *peem-yentos re-yehnos* stuffed peppers
pinchos morunos *peenchos moroonos* kebabs
pisto *peesto* fried peppers, onions, tomatoes and courgettes
plátanos *platanos* bananas
pollo al ajillo *po-yo al a-Heeyo* fried chicken with garlic
pollo asado *po-yo asado* roast chicken
pulpo *poolpo* octopus
puré de patata *pooreh deh patata* potato puré
purrusalda (sopa) *poorroosalda (sopa)* dried salted cod soup with leeks and potatoes

queso del país *kehso del pa-ees* local cheese
queso manchego *kehso manchehgo* hard, strong cheese from La Mancha
quisquillas *keeskeeyas* shrimps

rábanos *rabanos* radishes
ración de ... *rath-yon deh* portion of ...
rape a la cazuela *rapeh a la kathwehla* monkfish casserole
remolacha *rehmolacha* beetroot
riñones al jerez *reen-yones al Hereth* kidneys in a sherry sauce

salchichas *salcheechas* sausages
salchichón *salcheechon* salami-type sausage
salmón (ahumado) *salmon (ah-oomado)* (smoked) salmon
salmonetes *salmonehtes* red mullet
salpicón de mariscos *salpeekon deh mareeskos* shellfish with vinaigrette
salsa ali-oli *salsa alee-olee* garlic mayonnaise
salsa de tomate *salsa deh tomateh* tomato sauce
sardinas a la brasa *sardeenas a la brasa* barbecued sardines
sesos rebozados *sesos rebothados* brains fried in batter

solomillo con patatas fritas *solomeeyo kon patatas freetas* fillet steak with French fries

sopa de ajo *sopa deh a-Ho* bread and garlic soup

sopa de almendra *sopa deh almendra* marzipan-based pudding

sopa del día *sopa del dee-a* soup of the day

sopa de fideos *sopa deh feedeh-os* noodle soup

sopa de marisco *sopa deh mareesko* shellfish soup

sopa de pescado *sopa deh peskado* fish soup

tallarines *ta-yareenes* tagliatelle

tarta al whisky *tarta al weeskee* whisky-flavoured ice-cream gateau

tarta de almendra *tarta deh almendra* almond tart or gateau

tarta de chocolate *tarta deh chokolateh* chocolate gateau

tarta de manzana *tarta deh manthana* apple tart

tarta helada *tarta ehlada* ice-cream gateau

ternera asada *ternaira asada* roast veal

tocinillo de cielo *totheeneeyo deh th-yehlo* rich, thick crème caramel

tortilla de bonito *torteeya deh boneeto* tuna fish omelette

tortilla de patata *torteeya patata* potato omelette

tortilla española *torteeya espan-yola* potato omelette

tortilla francesa *torteeya franthesa* plain omelette

tostón asado *toston asado* roast sucking pig

trucha (escabechada) *troocha (eskabechada)* (marinated) trout

turrón *toorron* nougat (eaten at Christmas)

zarzuela de mariscos *tharthwehla deh mareeskos* seafood stew

MONEY

(*see also BANKS*)

How much is it/how much is this?
¿Cuánto es/cuánto cuesta?
kwanto es/kwanto kwesta

What does that come to?
¿Cuánto le debo?
kwanto leh dehbo

Could you write that down?
¿Puede escribirlo?
pwehdeh eskreebeerlo

RESPONSE

Son quinientas pesetas, por favor.
son keen-yentas pesehtas por favor
That'll be 500 pesetas, please.

Can I use this credit card?
¿Puedo pagar con esta tarjeta de crédito?
pwehdo pagar kon esta tarHehta deh krehdeeto

Can I have the bill please?
¿Me trae la cuenta, por favor?
meh tra-eh la kwenta por favor

No I'll pay.
No, pago yo.
no pago yo

Can we pay together?
¿Nos hace la cuenta de todo junto?
nos atheh la kwenta deh todo Hoonto

Can we pay separately?
¿Nos hace la cuenta por separado?
nos atheh la kwenta por separado

Keep the change.
Quédese con el cambio.
kehdeseh kon el kamb-yo

Call it 3,000.
Quédese con las tres mil.
kehdehseh kon las tres meel

That's not right surely.
Eso debe de ser un error.
eso dehbeh deh sair oon error

That's too expensive.
Eso es carísimo.
eso es kareeseemo

Can you give me coins for this?
¿Me puede cambiar esto en monedas?
meh pwehdeh kamb-yar esto en monehdas

I'm broke.
Estoy sin blanca.
estoy seen blanka

He's loaded.
Está forrado.
esta forrado

Can I have a refund?
¿Me puede devolver el dinero?
meh pwehdeh dehbolbair el deenehro

MONTHS

January	**enero**	*enehro*
February	**febrero**	*febrehro*
March	**marzo**	*martho*
April	**abril**	*abreel*
May	**mayo**	*miyo*
June	**junio**	*ноon-yo*
July	**julio**	*ноol-yo*
August	**agosto**	*agosto*
September	**se(p)tiembre**	*se(p)t-yembreh*
October	**octubre**	*oktoobreh*
November	**noviembre**	*nob-yembreh*
December	**diciembre**	*deeth-yembreh*

This month.
Este mes.
esteh mehs

Next month.
El mes que viene.
el mehs keh b-yeneh

Last month.
El mes pasado.
el mehs pasado

In March/August.
En marzo/agosto.
en martho/agosto

In the summer months.
En los meses de verano.
en los mehses deh bairano

During the winter months.
Durante los meses de invierno.
dooranteh los mehses deh eenb-yairno

NECESSITY, OBLIGATION

Do I have to ...?
¿Tengo que ... ?
ten-go keh

We have to go now.
Tenemos que irnos ya.
tenehmos keh eernos ya

Is it necessary to pay in advance?
¿Hay que pagar por adelantado?
i keh pagar por adehlantado

That's not necessary.
No es necesario.
no es nethesar-yo

When do we have to be back by?
¿Cuándo tenemos que estar de vuelta?
kwando tenehmos keh estar deh bwelta

You must ...
Tienes/tiene que ...
t-yenes/t-yeneh keh

You must not ...
No tienes/tiene que ...
no t-yenes/t-yeneh keh

It must be ready tomorrow.
Tiene que estar listo para mañana.
t-yeneh keh estar leesto para man-yana

You shouldn't do that.
No deberías/debería hacer eso.
no debairee-as/debairee-a athair eso

NEGATIVES

To express a negative in Spanish, to say 'I DON'T want', 'it's NOT here' etc, you use the word **no** placed before the verb:

I want to. **Quiero.** *k-yehro*	I don't want to. **No quiero.** *no k-yehro*
She's here. Está aquí. *esta akee*	**She's not here.** No está aquí. *no esta akee*
I bought it. Lo compré. *lo kompreh*	**I didn't buy it.** No lo compré. *no lo kompreh*
It's going to rain. Va a llover. *ba a yobair*	**It's not going to rain.** No va a llover. *no ba a yobair*

Unlike English, Spanish makes use of double negatives:

I don't see anyone.
No veo a nadie.
no beh-o a nad-yeh (**nadie** − nobody)

They don't have any.
No tienen ninguno.
no t-yehnen neengoono (**ninguno** − none)

To say 'no sugar' etc make the accompanying verb
negative:

There's no sugar.
No hay azúcar.
no i athookar

I've no cigarettes.
No tengo cigarrillos.
no ten-go theegarree-yos

To say 'not her', 'not them' etc just use the relevant
personal pronoun followed by **no**:

Not them.
Ellos no
eh-yos no

Not her.
Ella no.
eh-ya no

NUMBERS

0	cero	*thehro*
1	uno	*oono*
2	dos	*dos*
3	tres	*très*
4	cuatro	*kwatro*
5	cinco	*theenko*
6	seis	*says*
7	siete	*s-yehteh*
8	ocho	*ocho*
9	nueve	*nwehbeh*
10	diez	*d-yeth*
11	once	*ontheh*
12	doce	*dotheh*
13	trece	*trehtheh*
14	catorce	*katortheh*
15	quince	*keentheh*
16	dieciséis	*d-yethee-says*
17	diecisiete	*d-yetheesee-ehteh*
18	dieciocho	*d-yethee-ocho*
19	diecinueve	*d-yethee-nwehbeh*
20	veinte	*baynteh*
21	veintiuno	*bayntee-oono*
22	veintidós	*bayntee-dos*
23	veintitrés	*bayntee-tres*
30	treinta	*traynta*
40	cuarenta	*kwarenta*
50	cincuenta	*theenkwenta*
60	sesenta	*sesenta*
70	setenta	*setenta*
80	ochenta	*ochenta*
90	noventa	*nobenta*
100	cien	*th-yen*
110	ciento diez	*th-yento-d-yeth*
200	doscientos	*dos-th-yentos*
300	trescientos	*tres-th-yentos*
500	quinientos	*keen-yentos*

1,000	**mil**	*meel*
2,000	**dos mil**	*dos meel*
1,000,000	**un millón**	*oon meeyon*

87 plus 36.
Ochenta y siete más treinta y seis.
ochenta ee s-yehteh mas traynta ee says

800 minus 132.
Ochocientos menos ciento treinta y dos.
ocho-th-yentos menos th-yento traynta ee dos

22 times 15.
Veintidós por quince.
baynteedos por keentheh

134 divided by 3.
Ciento treinta y cuatro entre tres.
th-yento traynta ee kwatro entreh tres

Fourteen and a half.
Catorce y medio.
katortheh ee mehd-yo

Twelve and a quarter.
Doce y cuarto.
dotheh ee kwarto

Twelve and three quarters.
Doce y tres cuartos.
dotheh ee tres kwartos

35 point five, 35.5.
Treinta y cinco coma cinco, 35,5.
traynta ee theenko koma theenko

36 point seven five.
Treinta y seis coma setenta y cinco.
traynta ee says koma setenta ee theenko

10%.
Diez por ciento.
d-yeth por th-yento

Half as much.
La mitad.
la meetad

How many?
¿Cuántos/cuántas?
kwantos/kwantas

How much?
¿Cuánto?
kwanto

More than 500.
Más de 500.
mas deh keen-yentos

Less than 50.
Menos de cincuenta.
mehnos deh theenkwenta

OFFERING

Can I help?
¿Puedo ayudar?
pwehdo a-yoodar

Let me.
Permítame.
pairmeeta-meh

May I ...?
¿Me permite ...?
meh pairmeeteh

I'll do that for you.
Yo te/se lo hago.
yo teh/seh lo ago

It's no problem.
No hay problema.
no i problehma

My pleasure.
Es un placer.
es oon plathair

Would you like one?
¿Quieres/quiere uno?
k-yehres/k-yehreh oono

Please take one.
Tome/toma uno.
tomeh/toma oono

Please, go on.
Por favor.
por favor

Take mine.
Tome/toma el mío.
tomeh/toma el mee-o

PAST TENSE

To put something into the past tense, to say that you HAVE DONE or DID DO something, you remove the **-ar**, **-er** or **-ir** endings from the infinitive of the verb (as given in the dictionary section of this book) and add the appropriate endings.

habl-é	*ableh*	I spoke
habl-aste	*ablasteh*	you spoke
habl-ó	*ablo*	he/she spoke, you spoke (*polite*)
habl-amos	*ablamos*	we spoke
habl-asteis	*ablastays*	you spoke
habl-aron	*ablaron*	they spoke, you spoke (*polite*)
com-í	*komee*	I ate
com-iste	*komeesteh*	you ate
com-ió	*kom-yo*	he/she ate, you ate (*polite*)
com-imos	*komeemos*	we ate
com-isteis	*komeestays*	you ate
com-ieron	*kom-yairon*	they ate, you ate (*polite*)
abr-í	*abree*	I opened
abr-iste	*abreesteh*	you opened
abr-ió	*abr-yo*	he/she opened, you opened (*polite*)
abr-imos	*abreemos*	we opened
abr-isteis	*abreestays*	you opened
abr-ieron	*abr-yairon*	they opened, you opened (*polite*)

Where did you buy that?
¿Dónde compraste eso?
dondeh komprasteh eso

I found it at the market.
Lo encontré en el mercado.
lo enkontreh en el merkado

We sold it.
Lo vendimos.
lo bendeemos

Here are three other useful verbs in another past tense, the imperfect (WAS etc and HAD). (For the difference between **ser** and **estar** see BE):

ser (to be)

era	*era*	I was
eras	*eras*	you were
era	*era*	he/she/it was, you were (*polite*)
éramos	*eramos*	we were
erais	*erīs*	you were
eran	*eran*	they were, you were (*polite*)

estar (to be)

estaba	*estaba*	I was
estabas	*estabas*	you were
estaba	*estaba*	he/she/it was, you were (*polite*)
estábamos	*estabamos*	we were
estabais	*estabís*	you were
estaban	*estaban*	they were, you were (*polite*)

tener (to have)

tenía	*tenee-a*	I had
tenías	*tenee-as*	you had
tenía	*tenee-a*	he/she/it had, you had (*polite*)
teníamos	*tenee-amos*	we had
teníais	*tenee-īs*	you had
tenían	*tenee-an*	they had, you had (*polite*)

PERMISSION

Can I ...?
¿Puedo ... ?
pwehdo

Can we ...?
¿Podemos ... ?
podehmos

Can he/she ...?
¿Puede ... ?
pwehdeh

Can they ...?
¿Pueden ... ?
pwehden

Can I go in?
¿Puedo pasar?
pwehdo pasar

Is it allowed?
¿Está permitido?
esta pairmeeteedo

Is that all right?
¿No (te/le) importa?
no (teh/leh) eemporta

Can you give me a permit?
¿Me pueden dar un permiso?
meh pwehden dar oon pairmeeso

That's ok, on you go.
Está bien, adelante.
esta b-yen adelanteh

PHOTOGRAPHS

Do you have a film for this camera?
¿Tiene un carrete para esta máquina?
t-yeneh oon karrehteh para esta makeena

35mm/16mm.
De 35mm/16 mm.
deh traynta-eetheenko/d-yethee-says meeleemetros

12/24/36 exposures.
De 12/24/36 exposiciones.
deh dotheh/baynteekwatro/traynta-ee-says exposeeth-yones

Can you develop these?
¿Puede revelarlos?
pwehdeh rebelarlos

I'd like prints/slides.
Queria fotos/diapositivas.
kehree-a fotos/deea-poseeteebas

Can you give me another print of these two?
¿Puede hacer una copia de estas dos?
pwehdeh athair oona kop-ya deh estas dos

Excuse me, could you take a photograph of me/us?
Por favor, ¿le importaría hacerme/hacernos una foto?
por favor leh eemportareea athairmeh/athairnos oona foto

Smile!
¡Una sonrisa!
oona sonreesa

YOU'LL SEE

Revelado de fotos.
rebelado deh fotos
Film processing.

Se hacen fotos en el acto.
seh athen fotos en el akto
Instant developing.

PLURALS

If a Spanish noun ends in a vowel, you form the plural by adding **-s**:

El chico.	**Los chicos.**
el cheeko	*los cheekos*
The boy.	The boys.
La botella.	**Las botellas.**
la boteh-ya	*las boteh-yas*
The bottle.	The bottles.

To form the plural of a word ending in a consonant, add **-es**:

El motor.	**Los motores.**
el motor	*los motores*
The engine.	The engines.
La estación.	**Las estaciones.**
la estath-yon	*las estath-yones*
The station.	The stations.

To form the plural of words ending in a **-z**, change the **-z** to **-ces**:

La luz.	**Las luces.**
la looth	*las loothess*
The light.	The lights.

See also ADJECTIVES.

POLICE AND THE LAW

(see also CAR ACCIDENTS, THEFT)

Could you come with me, there's been a fight.
¿Podría acompañarme? ha habido una pelea.
podree-a akompan-yarmeh a abeedo oona peleh-a

He started it.
Empezó él.
empetho el

It wasn't my fault.
No fue culpa mía.
no fweh koolpa mee-a

It was his/her fault.
Fue culpa suya.
fweh koolpa sooya

RESPONSES

¿Su nombre?
soo nombreh
Your name?

¿Su dirección?
soo deerekth-yon
Your address?

¿Me permite el pasaporte?
meh pairmeeteh el pasaporteh
Can I see your passport?

El carnet de identidad.
el karneh deh eedenteedad
Identity card.

I didn't know it wasn't allowed.
No sabía que no estaba permitido.
no sabee-a keh no estaba pairmeeteedo

There's no sign up.
No hay ninguna indicación.
no ī neengoona eendeekath-yon

It's not mine, I rented it.
No es mío, es alquilado.
no es mee-o es alkeelado

I want to report a loss.
Quería denunciar una pérdida.
kehree-a dehnoonth-yar oona pairdeeda

... has gone missing.
... ha desaparecido.
... a desaparetheedo

He/she was wearing ...
Llevaba ...
yehbaba

He/she has blue/brown eyes.
Tiene los ojos azules/castaños.
t-yeneh los oHos athooles/kastan-yos

He/she has blonde/red hair.
Es rubio(a)/pelirrojo(a)
es roob-yo(a)/pehleerroHo(a)

POSSESSIVES

If you want to say that something is YOUR car or HIS car or HER car etc then you use the following words in Spanish. Notice that there are several forms: one for masculine singular nouns (eg **el libro**); one for feminine singular nouns (eg **la idea**); one for masculine plural nouns (eg **los padres**); and one for feminine plural nouns (eg **las amigas**). In other words, possessive adjectives in Spanish agree in number and gender with the noun they accompany.

The forms are as follows:

	singular		*plural*	
	masc	*fem*	*masc*	*fem*
my	**mi**	**mi**	**mis**	**mis**
your	**tu**	**tu**	**tus**	**tus**
his/her/ its/your *(pol)*	**su**	**su**	**sus**	**sus**
our	**nuestro**	**nuestra**	**nuestros**	**nuestras**
your	**vuestro**	**vuestra**	**vuestros**	**vuestras**
their/your *(pol)*	**su**	**su**	**sus**	**sus**

Tu idea.
too eedeh-a
Your idea.

Sus padres.
soos padres
His/her/your parents.

Vuestra casa.
bwestra kasa
Your house.

Nuestros libros.
nwestros leebros
Our books.

To avoid the confusion often caused by the many uses of **su** and **sus**, it is helpful to place the following *after* the noun instead of using **su** or **sus** in front of the noun:

de él	his
de ella	her
de usted	your *(singular polite)*

de ellos	their
de ellas	their
de ustedes	your (*plural polite*)

El teléfono de usted.
el telefono deh oostehd
Your telephone.

La clase de ella.	**Los amigos de él.**
la klaseh deh eh-ya	*los ameegos deh el*
Her class.	His friends.

To say that something is YOURS or HERS you use one of the following, which, as with possessive adjectives, have to agree with what they refer to:

mine
| **el mío** | **la mía** | **los míos** | **las mías** |

yours
| **el tuyo** | **la tuya** | **los tuyos** | **las tuyas** |

his/hers
| **el suyo** | **la suya** | **los suyos** | **las suyas** |

yours (*pol*)
| **el suyo** | **la suya** | **los suyos** | **las suyas** |

ours
| **el nuestro** | **la nuestra** | **los nuestros** | **las nuestras** |

yours
| **el vuestro** | **la vuestra** | **los vuestros** | **las vuestras** |

theirs
| **el suyo** | **la suya** | **los suyos** | **las suyas** |

yours (*pol*)
| **el suyo** | **la suya** | **los suyos** | **las suyas** |

No es mi bolsa, es la suya.
no es mee bolsa es la sooya
It isn't my bag, it's yours.

No son las nuestras, son las de su hermana.
no son las nwestras son las deh soo airmana
They're not ours, they're his sister's.

POSSIBILITIES

Is it possible to ...?
¿Se puede ... ?
seh pwehdeh

Could I possibly borrow this?
¿Cree que podría llevarme esto prestado?
kreh-eh keh podree-a yehbarmeh esto prestado

I might, I'm not sure.
Quizás, no estoy seguro.
keethas no estoy segooro

We might want to stay longer.
Puede que queramos quedarnos más tiempo.
pwehdeh keh keramos kehdarnos mas t-yempo

He might have.
Es posible.
es poseebleh

They might have left already.
Puede que ya se hayan marchado.
pwehdeh keh ya seh iyan marchado

Who knows?
¡Quién sabe!
k-yen sabeh

There's an outside chance.
Existe una remota posibilidad.
exeesteh oona remota poseebeeleedad

That's out of the question!
¡Ni pensarlo!
nee pensar-lo

POST OFFICE

Two stamps for letters to the UK please.
¿Me da dos sellos de carta para Gran Bretaña?
meh da dos sehyos deh karta para gran bretan-ya

Eight stamps for postcards to England please.
¿Me da ocho sellos de postal para Inglaterra?
meh da ocho seh-yos deh postal para eenglaterra

Do you have three air-mail envelopes?
¿Me da tres sobres por avión?
meh da tres sobres por ab-yon

I'd like to send this registered.
Quería enviar esto certificado.
keree-a enb-yar esto thairteefeekado

Is there any mail for me?
¿Hay correo para mí?
i korreh-o para mee

YOU'LL SEE

Sellos.
seh-yos
Stamps.

Apartado de Correos.
apartado deh korreh-os
PO Box.

Lista de Correos.
leesta deh korreh-os
Poste Restante.

Extranjero.
extranHehro
Overseas.

PRACTISING YOUR SPANISH

Here are twenty questions about Spanish. All of them can be answered by using the information given in the various sections of this book. The answers are on the next page.

1. What are the two Spanish verbs for 'to be'?
2. What is the plural of **la farmacia/el bonbón**?
3. What is the Spanish for 'we can'?
4. **Estoy cansado** means 'I am tired'. What is 'I am not tired'?
5. If you are a woman, how do you say 'I am tired?'
6. How do you say 'of the hotel/to the hotel'?
7. **Usted** is the polite pronoun for 'you'. What is the familiar pronoun?
8. **Fácil** means 'easy'. How do you say 'easier'?
9. How do you say 'faster than the bus'?
10. What is the Spanish for 'on Tuesdays'?
11. What do the signs **salida/se ruega no ...** mean?
12. If you order a **café solo** to drink what will you get?
13. How would you ask for a single room for two nights?
14. How do you ask for the bill in a restaurant?
15. What is **pollo**?
16. **Estoy muy contento** means 'I'm very pleased'. Say 'I was very pleased'.
17. How do you say 'I live in ...'?
18. How do you ask someone their name?
19. If someone says 'thanks very much' to you in Spanish what could you reply?
20. How do you pronounce **Marbella/zumo/niño/puedo**?

1. Ser and estar.
2. Las farmacias/los bonbones.
3. Podemos.
4. No estoy cansado.
5. Estoy cansada.
6. Del hotel/al hotel.
7. Tú.
8. Más fácil.
9. Más rápido que el autobús.
10. Los martes.
11. Exit/please do not.
12. A black coffee.
13. ¿Tiene una habitación individual para dos noches?
14. ¿Me trae la cuenta, por favor?
15. Chicken.
16. Estaba muy contento.
17. Vivo en . . .
18. ¿Cómo te llamas? or ¿Cómo se llama?
19. De nada.
20. *marbeh-ya/thoomo/neen-yo/pwehdo*

PRESENT TENSE

To form the present tense of a verb, to say that you ARE DOING something or that something HAPPENS, you take off the **-ar**, **-er** or **-ir** ending of the verb as given in the dictionary in this book and then add the following endings:

hablar (to speak)

habl-o	*ablo*	I speak
habl-as	*ablas*	you speak
habl-a	*abla*	he/she speaks, you speak
habl-amos	*ablamos*	we speak
habl-áis	*ablís*	you speak
habl-an	*ablan*	they speak, you speak

comer (to eat)

com-o	*komo*	I eat
com-es	*komes*	you eat
com-e	*komeh*	he/she eats, you eat
com-emos	*komehmos*	we eat
com-éis	*komays*	you eat
com-en	*komen*	they eat, you eat

abrir (to open)

abr-o	*abro*	I open
abr-es	*abres*	you open
abr-e	*abreh*	he/she opens, you open
abr-imos	*abreemos*	we open
abr-ís	*abrees*	you open
abr-en	*abren*	they open, you open

Note that this tense also translates English uses such as I AM SPEAKING etc.

The most common irregular verbs are:

tenir	venir	ir	dar
(to have)	(to come)	(to go)	(to give)
tengo	vengo	voy	doy
tienes	vienes	vas	das
tiene	viene	va	da
tenemos	venimos	vamos	damos
tenéis	venís	vais	dais
tienen	vienen	van	dan

The following verbs are irregular in the I form only:

decir	(to say)	digo
hacer	(to do, to make)	hago
poner	(to put)	pongo
sabor	(to know)	sé
salir	(to go out)	salgo

Two other useful verbs in the present tense are:

poder (to be able)

puedo	*pwehdo*	I can
puedes	*pwehdehs*	you can
puede	*pwehdeh*	he/she/it can, you can (*polite*)
podemos	*podehmos*	we can
podéis	*podays*	you can
pueden	*pwehden*	they can, you can (*polite*)

querer (to want)

quiero	*k-yehro*	I want
quieres	*k-yehres*	you want
quiere	*k-yehreh*	he/she/it wants, you want (*polite*)
queremos	*kairehmos*	we want
queréis	*kairays*	you want
quieren	*k-yehren*	they want, you want (*polite*)

104

PRONOUNS

Subject pronouns are:

yo	*yo*	I
tú	*too*	you
él	*el*	he/it
ella	*eh-ya*	she/it
usted	*oostehd*	you (*polite*)
nosotros	*nosotros*	we
vosotros	*bosotros*	you
ellos	*eh-yos*	they (*masculine*)
ellas	*eh-yas*	they (*feminine*)
ustedes	*oostehdes*	you (*polite*)

Personal pronouns as subjects are rarely needed in Spanish, since the ending of the verb (and the context) usually make things clear:

I don't know.   **Where are we?**
No sé.   ¿Dónde estamos?
no say   *dondeh estamos*

Typical uses of these forms are shown in the following examples:

Who did it? — I did/I didn't.
¿Quién lo hizo? — Lo hice yo/no lo hice yo.
k-yen lo eetho — lo eetheh yo/no lo eetheh yo

It's him/us
Es él/somos nosotros.
es el/somos nosotros

Are you coming too?
¿Vienes tú/viene usted también?
b-yehnes too/b-yehneh oostehd tamb-yehn

Me, I don't want to.
Yo no quiero.
yo no k-yehro

The pronouns as listed above are also used after prepositions:

For you.
Para usted.
para oostehd

With her.
Con ella.
kon eh-ya

Without him.
Sín él.
seen el

After us.
Después de nosotros.
despwehs deh nosotros

But **yo** changes to **mí** and **tú** changes to **ti**:

That's for me/you.
Eso es para mí/ti.
eso es para mee/tee

There are also two special changes after **con** (with):

With me/you.
Conmigo/contigo.
konmeego/konteego

YOU: tú is used when speaking to someone who is a friend or to someone of your own general age group with whom you want to establish a friendly atmosphere. **Vosotros'** is used when speaking to several friends (it is the plural of **tú**).

Usted and **ustedes** are used when speaking to someone you don't know. In the vast majority of cases when travelling as a foreigner in Spain you will use the **usted** form. Certainly if you are in any doubt as to which form to use, choose the **usted** form. When using **usted** and **ustedes** the verbs have the same endings as for 'he/she and they'.

If you are using the pronoun as an object, saying 'I know HIM' or 'he saw THEM' etc, use the following words:

me	*meh*	me
te	*teh*	you
le	*leh*	him, you (*polite*)
lo	*lo*	it
la	*la*	her/it, you (*polite*)
nos	*nos*	us
os	*os*	you
les/los	*les/los*	them, you (*polite*)
las	*las*	them, you (*polite*)

I know him.
Le conozco.
leh konothko

He saw them.
Los vió.
los b-yo

Can you hear me?
¿Me oyes?
meh o-yes

Can you help us?
¿Puede ayudarnos?
pwehdeh a-yoodarnos

Puedo hacerlo mañana.
pwehdo athairlo man-yana
I can do it tomorrow.

If you are using a pronoun to say, for example, you sent something 'TO HER' or that you spoke 'TO HIM', then use the following words:

me	*meh*	to me
te	*teh*	to you
le/se	*leh/seh*	to him/to her, to you (*polite*)
nos	*nos*	to us
os	*os*	to you
les	*les*	to them, to you (*polite*)

I spoke to him.
Le hablé.
leh ableh

He gave it to me/him.
Me/se lo dio.
meh lo d-yo

PRONUNCIATION

As compared with English, Spanish is a very regular language when it comes to pronunciation. The following general guidelines to special sounds will help you pronounce new Spanish words that you encounter. To get the actual values of the sounds listen carefully to a Spanish speaker and try to copy what you hear.(*See also the INTRODUCTION*).

ai, ay	like the i in hide (baile, hay)
au	ow as in cow (autobús)
ce, ci	as th in thumb (centro, cinco)
d	when not at the beginning of a word is softer than English d, between d and th (cada, llegada, usted)
ei, ey	as ey in they (reina, ley)
eu	ay-oo (deuda)
ge, gi	like the ch in the Scottish pronunciation of loch (general, gitano)
h	is always silent
ie	like ye in yellow (nieve, cielo)
j	like the ch in the Scottish pronunciation of loch (patinaje)
ll	like the y in yes (llamar, cepillo, pollo)
ñ	like ni in onion (riñón, niño)
oi, oy	oy as in boy (hoy, oigo)
qu	like the k in king (que, querida)
r	is more rolled than the English r (rubia)
rr	very strongly rolled
ue	as in way (vuelo, nuevo)
v	something like the b in boy (voy, verano)
y	either as in yes (vaya) or, if by itself, ee as in seen (y), see also ey, oy
z	th as in thumb (zumo, caza)

QUESTIONS

What is ...?
¿Qué es/está ...?
keh es/esta

Where is ...?
¿Dónde es/está ... ?
dondeh es/esta

When is ...?
¿Cuándo es/está ... ?
kwando es/esta

Which is ...?
¿Cuál es/está ...?
kwal es/esta

Who is ...?
¿Quién es/está ...?
k-yen es/esta

Why is ...?
¿Por qué es/está ...?
por keh es/esta

How long will it take?
¿Cuánto tardará?
kwanto tardara

How do I get to ...?
¿Cómo se va a ...?
komo seh ba a

How do you do it?
¿Cómo se hace?
komo seh atheh

What are these?
¿Qué son éstos?
keh son estos

Where are we going?
¿Dónde vamos?
dondeh bamos

Which are mine?
¿Cuáles son los míos?
kwales son los meeos

Can you tell me ...?
¿Me puede decir ...?
meh pwehdeh detheer

Can you ...?
¿Puedes/puede ...?
pwehdes/pwehdeh

Can I ...?
¿Puedo ...?
pwehdo

Can we ...?
¿Podemos ...?
podehmos

Can he/she ...?
¿Puede ...?
pwehdeh

Could you write it down?
¿Podría escribirlo?
podree-a eskreebeerlo

REFERRING TO THINGS/PEOPLE

This.
Esto.
esto

That.
Eso.
eso

This car, this one.
Este coche, éste.
esteh kocheh esteh

That car, that one.
Ese coche, ése.
eseh kocheh eseh

This house, this one.
Esta casa, ésta.
esta kasa esta

That house, that one.
Esa casa, ésa.
esa kasa esa

That one (over there).
Aquél/aquélla.
akel/akeh-ya

Not that one, the one behind it.
Ése no, el de más atrás.
eseh no el deh mas atras

That one over there.
Aquél de allá.
akel deh iya

The man over there.
Aquel hombre de allá.
akel ombreh deh iya

Him, her.
El, ella.
el eh-ya

Him in the green shirt.
El de la camisa verde.
el deh la kameesa bairdeh

The woman next to her.
La señora que está a su lado.
la sen-yora keh esta a soo lado

These two, those two.
Estos dos, ésos dos/aquéllos dos.
estos dos esos dos/akeh-yos dos

No no, the other one.
No, no, el otro.
no no el otro

RENTALS

I want to hire a car/moped.
Quiero alquilar un coche/una motocicleta.
k-yehro alkeelar oon kocheh/oona mototheeklehta

Can I rent one for a day/two days/a week?
¿Puedo alquilar uno por un día/dos días/una semana?
pwehdo alkeelar oono por oon dee-a/dos dee-as/oona semana

How much is it per day?
¿Cuánto cuesta al día?
kwanto kwesta al dee-a

When do we have to bring it back?
¿Cuándo tenemos que devolverlo?
kwando tenehmos keh dehbolbairlo

RESPONSES

Su permiso de conducir, por favor.
soo pairmeeso deh kondootheer por favor
Your driving licence please.

Su pasaporte, por favor.
soo pasaporteh por favor
Your passport please.

¿Dónde se aloja?
dondeh seh aloнa
Where are you staying?

I'm at the ... Hotel.
Estoy en el Hotel ...
estoy en el otel

It's rented.
Es alquilado.
es alkeelado

112

REPAIRS

Can you fix this?
¿Puede arreglar esto?
pwehdeh arreglar esto

It's broken.
Se ha roto.
seh a roto

Can you put new soles on these?
¿Les puede poner suelas nuevas?
les pwehdeh ponair swehlas nwehbas

Can you re-heel these?
¿Les puede poner tacones?
les pwehdeh ponair takones

Can you put a patch on this?
¿Le puede poner un parche a esto?
leh pwehdeh ponair oon parcheh a esto

Can you replace this?
¿Puede poner uno nuevo?
pwehdeh ponair oono nwehbo

It needs a new . . .
Necesita un . . . nuevo.
netheseeta oon . . . nwehbo

Can you do it today/by tomorrow?
¿Puede tenerlo para hoy/para mañana?
pwehdeh tenairlo para oy/para man-yana

Can you write the price down?
¿Puede anotar el importe?
pwehdeh anotar el eemporteh

REQUESTS

Could you please ...?
¿Me haría el favor de ...?
meh aree-a el favor deh

Could you tell me ...?
¿Me podría decir ...?
meh podree-a detheer

Could you give this to her?
¿Podría darle esto?
podree-a darleh esto

Could I ...?
¿Podría ...?
podree-a

Could I have one?
¿Puedes/puede darme uno?
pwehdes/pwehdeh darmeh oono

Could we have another?
¿Puedes/puede darnos otro?
pwehdehs/pwehdeh darnos otro

Please leave it open.
Por favor, déjalo/déjelo abierto.
por favor deHalo/deHelo ab-yerto

Please don't.
No, por favor.
no por favor

Please don't speak so fast.
Por favor, no hables/hable tan deprisa.
por favor no ables/ableh tan deh-preesa

RESTAURANTS

(see MENU READER and DICTIONARY)

A table for one/two please.
Una mesa para una persona/dos, por favor.
oona mehsa para oona pairsona/dos por favor

Can we have a table outside/inside?
¿Nos podría poner en una mesa de fuera/dentro?
nos podree-a ponair en oona mehsa deh fwehra/dentro

Can I book a table for this evening?
¿Podría reservar mesa para esta noche?
podree-a reserbar mehsa para esta nocheh

I've booked a table.
He reservado mesa.
eh reserbado mehsa

The name is . . .
A nombre de . . .
a nombreh deh

Can I see the menu?
¿Me trae la carta?
meh tra-eh la karta

Can I see the wine list please?
Por favor, ¿me trae la carta de vinos?
por favor meh tra-eh la karta deh beenos

Can we have the set menu for two?
¿Nos trae dos platos del día?
nos tra-eh dos platos del dee-a

A litre of house red please.
Una botella de tinto de la casa, por favor.
oona boteh-ya deh teento deh la kasa por favor

Half a litre of house white please.
Media botella de blanco de la casa, por favor
mehd-ya boteh-ya deh blanko deh la kasa por favor

Waiter!/miss!
¡Camarero!/¡señorita!
kamarehro/sen-yoreeta

That's for me thanks.
Para mí, gracias.
para mee grath-yas

That's for him/her.
Para él/ella.
para el/eh-ya

I didn't order this.
Yo no he pedido esto.
yo no eh pedeedo esto

I ordered red wine.
Pedí vino tinto.
pedee beeno teento

I'm afraid this tastes funny.
Perdone, pero esto no sabe bien.
pairdoneh pairo esto no sabeh b-yen

Can we see the dessert trolley?
¿Podemos ver el carrito de los postres?
podehmos bair el karreeto deh los postres

Two coffees please.
Dos cafés, por favor.
dos kafehs por favor

A tea please.
Un té, por favor.
oon teh por favor

One white coffee and one black, please.
Un café con leche y un café solo, por favor.
oon kafeh kon lecheh ee oon kafeh solo por favor

That was absolutely excellent!
¡No podía haber estado mejor!
no podee-a abair estado meHor

Can I have the bill please?
¿Me trae la cuenta, por favor?
meh tra-eh la kwenta por favor

ROAD SIGNS

¡alto! stop
apague las luces switch off your lights
aparcamiento parking
aparcamiento vigilado supervised parking
autopista (de peaje) (toll) motorway
callejón sin salida cul-de-sac
cambio de sentido take filter lane to exit and cross flow of traffic
camino cerrado (al tráfico) road closed (to traffic)
carretera cortada road blocked
carretera de circunvalación by-pass
carretera de doble calzada dual carriageway
ceda el paso give way
centro urbano/ciudad city/town centre
conduzca con cuidado drive with care
cruce de ganado danger: cattle crossing
curva peligrosa dangerous bend
desviación, desvío diversion
dirección única one way traffic
disco obligatorio parking disk must be displayed
encienda las luces switch on your lights
estacionamiento limitado restricted parking
estrechamiento de calzada road narrows
final de autopista end of motorway
firme deslizante slippery surface
gravilla loose chippings
límite de velocidad speed limit
luz de cruce use dipped headlights
obras roadworks
paso a nivel level crossing
paso de peatones pedestrian crossing
paso subterráneo underpass
peatón camine por la izquierda pedestrians please keep to the left
peligro de incendio fire hazard
prohibido tocar la bocina/el claxon do not sound your horn
reduzca la velocidad reduce speed now
salida de camiones lorry exit
vehículos pesados heavy vehicles
velocidad limitada speed limits apply
zona reservada para peatones pedestrian precinct

ROOMS – FINDING A ROOM

(*see also HOTELS*)

I'm looking for a room.
Estoy buscando alojamiento.
estoy booskando aloHam-yento

Where can I find a room that's not too expensive?
¿Dónde podría encontrar una habitación que no fuese muy cara?
dondeh podree-a enkontrar oona abeetath-yon keh no fwehseh mwee kara

What's a good area for finding a room?
¿Qué zona es buena para encontrar alojamiento?
keh thona es bwena para enkontrar aloHam-yento

Just one night/three nights.
Sólo una noche/tres noches.
solo oona nocheh/tres noches

Just one person/there are two of us.
Para una persona sola/somos dos.
para oona pairsona sola/somos dos

Could you write the address down for me?
¿Me podría escribir la dirección?
meh podree-a eskreebeer la deerekth-yon

Could you ring them from here to check?
¿Podría llamarles desde aquí para comprobar?
podree-a yamarles dezdeh akee para komprobar

> **La ciudad está llena hasta los topes.**
> *la th-yoodad esta yehna asta los topes*
> The town is absolutely full up.

> **Intente ...**
> *eententeh*
> Try ...

SELF-CATERING APARTMENTS

Could you check the cooker/fridge/shower?
¿Podría revisar la cocina/nevera/ducha?
podree-a rebeesar la kotheena/nebaira/doocha

How does the . . . work?
¿Cómo funciona el/la . . .?
komo foonth-yona el/la

The maid wasn't there today.
La chica no ha venido hoy.
la cheeka no ha beneedo oy

The people next door to us make a terrible noise.
Los de al lado arman muchísimo ruido.
los deh al lado arman moocheeseemo rweedo

Could you maybe have a quiet word with them?
¿No podría hablar con ellos?
no podree-a ablar kon eh-yos

When does the shop open/close?
¿A qué hora abre/cierra la tienda?
a keh ora abreh/th-yehra la t-yenda

Could we have some clean bedding?
¿Nos puede dar ropa de cama limpia?
nos pwehdeh dar ropa deh kama leemp-ya

Thank you for looking after us.
Gracias por sus cuidados.
grath-yas por soos kweedados

SHOPPING

I've got some shopping to do.
Tengo que hacer unas compras.
ten-go keh athair oonas kompras

He's gone to the shop.
Ha ido a la tienda.
a eedo a la t-yenda

Do you have . . . ?
¿Tiene . . . ?
t-yeneh

I'm just looking thanks.
Estoy viendo nada más, gracias.
estoy b-yendo nada mas grath-yas

Can I have a look around?
¿Puedo echar un vistazo?
pwehdo echar oon beestatho

How much is this?
¿Cuánto cuesta esto?
kwanto kwesta esto

Do you have other colours?
¿Lo tiene en otros colores?
lo t-yeneh en otros kolores

Do you have any smaller ones?
¿Lo tiene en más pequeño?
lo t-yeneh en mas pekehn-yo

Do you have any bigger ones?
¿Lo tiene en más grande?
lo t-yeneh en mas grandeh

It's not really what I was looking for.
No es exactamente lo que andaba buscando.
no es exactamenteh lo keh andaba booskando

That's fine, I'll take it.
Está bien, me lo llevo.
esta b-yen meh lo yehbo

Could you gift-wrap it for me?
¿Me lo puede envolver para regalo?
meh lo pwehdeh enbolbair para regalo

Can I use this credit card?
¿Puedo pagar con esta tarjeta de crédito?
pwehdo pagar kon esta tarHehta deh krehdeeto

SIGNS

Abierto.
ab-yerto
Open.

Cerrado.
thairrado
Closed.

Entrada libre.
entrada leebreh
No obligation to buy.

Precios de liquidación.
preth-yos deh leekeedath-yon
All prices slashed.

Rebajas.
rebaHas
Sale.

SIGHTSEEING

Do you have a map of the area?
¿Tiene un mapa de la zona?
t-yeneh oon mapa deh la thona

Do you have a guidebook for the area?
¿Tiene una guía de la zona?
t-yeneh oona gee-a deh la thona

Are there any guided sightseeing tours?
¿Hay excursiones organizadas?
i exkoors-yones organeethadas

We want to go to ...
Queremos ir a ...
kerehmos eer a

We've been seeing the sights.
Hemos estado viendo los lugares de interés turístico.
ehmos estado b-yendo los loogares deh eenteres tooreesteeko

I want to see the real Spain.
Quiero conocer la España auténtica.
k-yehro konothair la espan-ya owtenteeka

Can you give us the name of a really typical restaurant?
¿Nos puede indicar algún restaurante típico?
nos pwehdeh eendeekar algoon restowranteh teepeeko

SIGNS

Visitas con guía.
Beeseetas kon gee-a
Guided tours.

Zona monumental.
thona monoomental
Historic monuments.

122

SIGNS

abierto open
acceso a los andenes to the trains
aduana customs
agítese antes de usar shake before use
agua potable drinking water
albergue de juventud youth hostel
almuerzo lunch
alquiler de coches car rentals
ambulatorio national health clinic
andén platform
artículos de ocasión second hand goods
ascensor lift
aseos toilets
¡atención! take care
autoservicio self-service
aviso information
bienvenido welcome
bomberos fire brigade
buzón mail box
caballeros gentlemen
caduca ... expires ..., best before ...
caja cash desk
camarotes cabins
casa de socorro first aid centre
cena dinner
cerrado por obras/reforma closed for alteration/renovation
cerrado por vacaciones closed for holidays
CH, casa de huéspedes rooming house
comedor dining room
completo no vacancies
consérvese en sitio fresco store in a cool place
consigna left luggage
consúmase antes de ... best before ...
corrida de toros bull fight
cuidado con el escalón mind the step
cuidado con el perro beware of the dog
damas ladies
desayuno breakfast
desembarcadero quay
despacho de billetes ticket office
empujar push
entrada entrance

123

entrada libre admission free
entre sin llamar enter without knocking
escuela de párvulos kindergarten
es peligroso bañarse dangerous for swimming
espere please wait
esta tienda se traslada a ... business is being transferred to ...
fecha de caducidad expiry date
guardería (infantil) crèche
hostal-residencia long-stay boarding house
instituto de belleza beauty salon
IVA (impuesto sobre el valor añadido) VAT
lavar a mano wash by hand
lavar en seco dry clean
liquidación sale
lista de Correos poste restante
listas de bodas wedding lists
llegadas arrivals
llame al timbre please ring
marisquería shellfish bar
marroquinería fancy leather goods
metro underground
mirador scenic view
modo de empleo instructions for use
no funciona out of order
no se admiten caravanas no caravans allowed
no tocar please do not touch
ocupado engaged
oficina de objetos perdidos lost property office
ojo al tren beware of the train
oportunidades bargains
parada de autobús bus stop
parada de taxis taxi rank
parque de atracciones amusement park
peligro danger
piso floor
playa beach
policía police
prohibida la entrada no entry
prohibida la entrada a menores de ... no admission for those under ... years of age
prohibido asomarse do not lean out

prohibido el paso keep out
prohibido fumar no smoking
prohibido hablar con el conductor do not speak to the driver
prohibido pisar el césped/la hierba keep off the grass
prohibido tirar basura no litter
rebajas reductions
recién pintado wet paint
RENFE (red nacional de ferrocarriles españoles) Spanish railways
repuestos spares
reservado el derecho de admisión the management reserve the right to refuse admission
retraso delay
salida exit
salida de emergencia emergency exit
salidas departures
se aceptan tarjetas de crédito we accept credit cards
se alquila for hire, to rent
se hacen fotocopias photocopying service
señoras ladies
se ruega no . . . please do not . . .
servicios toilets
se vende for sale
sírvase please
sótano basement
tirar pull
tóxico poisonous
urbanización housing estate
Vd, Vds (usted, ustedes) you
venta de sellos stamps sold here
ventas al contado cash sales
ventas a plazos hire purchase
v.o. subtitulada original version with subtitles
zona monumental historic monuments

SMOKING

Can I have a packet of ...?
¿Me da un paquete de ...?
meh da oon pakehteh deh

Have you got a light?
¿Tienes/tiene fuego?
t-yenes/t-yeneh fwehgo

Do you mind if I smoke?
¿Te/le importa que fume?
teh/leh eemporta keh foomeh

Do you smoke?
¿Fumas?/¿fuma?
foomas/fooma

I've given up.
Lo he dejado.
lo eh deHado

Try one of these.
Prueba/pruebe uno de estos.
prwehba/prwehbeh oonó deh estos

Excuse me, it's no smoking here.
Perdone, pero esto es zona de no fumadores.
pairdoneh pairo esto es thona deh no foomadores

I quite enjoy the occasional cigar.
Me gusta fumar un puro de vez en cuando.
meh goosta foomar oon pooro deh beth en kwando

Do you have any pipe tobacco?
¿Tiene tabaco de pipa?
t-yeneh tabako deh peepa

SPAIN

With an area of some 505,000 square kilometres (as compared with the UK's 244,000) Spain is Western Europe's second largest country. It has a population of around 39 million (as compared with 56 million in the UK). The capital city of Madrid has a population of over 4,000,000 'madrileños'. Other major cities are Barcelona, Bilbao, Sevilla and Valencia.

Castilian Spanish is the official language, although other languages also enjoy official status in their own communities: Gallego in Galicia, Euskera in the Basque country and Catalán in Catalonia, Valencia and the Balearic Islands.

Spain is a parliamentary democracy with both a prime minister and a monarch.

Although perhaps best known for its seaside resorts, Spain is in fact a place of considerable geographical contrasts. In the Pyrenees there are soaring snow-covered peaks — Aneto rises to 3,404 metres and Monte Perdido to 3,353 metres. In the north the area along the Cantabrian coast is green and wet and hilly. To the south the Cantabrian mountains form the border with the huge central plateau of Spain, a place of cold winters and hot summers where vast plains dominate the landscape but where pockets of fertile ground are found along the banks of the rivers, the Duero and the Tajo (Tagus).

In the south the winters are mild and the summers very hot. Huge desert regions (Almeria) alternate with mountainous landscapes (Sierra Morena, Sierra Nevada — which has Spain's highest peak, the Mulhacén) and with fertile land where olive trees and orange trees grow in abundance.

The Canary Islands are the tropical part of Spain, dominated by the volcanic mass of Mount Teide.

SPORT

Let's go to the swimming baths.
Vamos a la piscina (cubierta).
bamos a la peestheena (koob-yairta)

Isn't there an outdoor pool?
¿No hay piscina?
no i peestheena

Is there a sports centre here?
¿Hay un polideportivo por aquí?
i oon poleedehporteebo por akee

I'm going jogging – coming too?
Voy a hacer footing – ¿vienes?
boy a athair footeeng – bee-ehnes

How about a game of tennis?
¿Y si jugáramos un partido de tenis?
ee see Hoogaramos oon parteedo deh tenees

Your serve.
Sacas tú/saca usted.
sakas too/saka oostehd

Good shot!
¡Buena jugada!
bwehna Hoogada

I'd like to hire a sailboard.
Quería alquilar una plancha.
kehree-a alkeelar oona plancha

Can we go sailing?
¿Podemos ir a hacer vela?
podehmos eer a athair behla

There's a football match on television.
Hay un partido de fútbol en la televisión.
i oon parteedo deh footbol en la telebees-yon

SUGGESTIONS

What do you suggest?
¿Qué propones/propone?
keh propones/proponeh

Let's go the beach/cinema.
¡Vamos a la playa/al cine!
bamos a la pliya/al theeneh

Let's leave.
Vámonos.
bamonos

How about an ice cream/a beer?
¿Nos tomamos un helado/una cerveza?
nos tomæmos oon ehlado/oona thairbehtha

Why don't we hire a car?
¿Por qué no alquilamos un coche?
por keh no alkeelamos oon kocheh

Why don't you talk to her?
¿Por qué no hablas/habla con ella?
por keh no ablas/abla kon eh-ya

Why don't you complain about it?
¿Por qué no vas/va a reclamar?
por keh no bas/ba a reklamar

You should tell the manager about it.
Deberías/debería hablar con el director.
debairee-as/debairee-a ablar kon el deerektor

How about it?, what do you say?
Y de eso ¿qué me dices/dice?
ee deh eso keh meh deethes/deetheh

SURPRISE

What a surprise!
¡Qué sorpresa!
keh sorprehsa

Well, look who it is!
¡Anda, mira quién está aquí!
anda meera k-yen esta akee

Well well well!
¡Vaya, vaya, vaya!
biya biya biya

Good heavens!
¡Santo cielo!
santo th-yehlo

Struth!
¡Por Dios!
por d-yos

That's amazing!
¡Es increíble!
es eenkreh-eebleh

That's terrible!
¡Qué horror!
keh orror

I don't believe it!
¡No me lo creo!
no meh lo kreh-o

How strange!
¡Qué raro!
keh raro

TALKING ABOUT ONESELF

My name is ...
Me llamo ...
meh yamo

I am ... years old.
Tengo ... años.
ten-go ... an-yos

I'm a teacher/doctor/taxi-driver.
Soy profesor/médico/taxista.
soy profesor/medeeko/taxeesta

I'm a hairdresser/nurse/teacher. (female)
Soy peluquera/enfermera/profesora.
soy pelookehra/enfairmehra/profesora

I come from England.
Soy inglés/inglesa.
soy eenglehs/eenglehsa

I was born in London/Ireland.
Nací en Londres/Irlanda.
nathee en londres/eerlanda

I was born in 1956.
Nací en mil novecientos cincuenta y seis.
nathee en meel nobeth-yentos theenkwenta ee says

I live in ...
Vivo en ...
beebo en

I'm single/married.
Estoy soltero(a)/casado(a).
estoy soltairo(a)/kasado(a)

I have two children.
Tengo dos hijos.
ten-go dos eeHos

I'm separated/I'm divorced.
Estoy separado(a)/divorciado(a).
estoy sehparado(a)/deeborth-yado(a)

TALKING TO PEOPLE

What's your name?
¿Cómo te llamas/se llama?
komo teh yamas/seh yama

How old are you?
¿Cuántos años tienes/tiene?
kwantos an-yos t-yenes/t-yeneh

What do you do?
¿A qué te dedicas/se dedica?
a keh teh dedeekas/seh dedeeka

Where do you come from?
¿De dónde eres/es?
deh dondeh ehres/es

Where do you live?
¿Dónde vives/vive?
dondeh beebes/beebeh

Are you married?
¿Estás/está casado(a)?
estas/esta kasado(a)

Do you have any family?
¿Tienes/tiene hijos?
t-yenes/t-yeneh eeHos

Have you ever been to Britain?
¿Has/ha estado en Gran Bretaña?
as/a estado en gran bretan-ya

Do you speak English?
¿Hablas/habla inglés?
ablas/abla eengles

TAXIS

Could you get me a taxi?
¿Me puede pedir un taxi?
meh pwehdeh pedeer oon taxee

I'd like to book a taxi for tomorrow morning.
Querría encargar un taxi para mañana por la mañana.
kehree-a enkargar oon taxee para man-yana por la man-yana

To the railway station/Prado museum.
A la estación de ferrocarril/al Museo del Prado.
a la estath-yon deh ferrokareel/al mooseh-o del prado

How much is it going to cost?
¿Cuánto va a costar?
kwanto ba a kostar

Could you stop here?
¿Puede parar aquí?
pwehdeh parar akee

This is fine.
Está bien.
esta b-yen

Can you wait here for me/us please?
¿Me/nos espera aquí, por favor?
meh/nos espehra akee por favor

Can you take me/us back again?
¿Me/nos puede llevar otra vez al sitio donde me/nos cogió?
meh/nos pwehdeh yevar otra beth al seet-yo dondeh me/nos koH-yo

Can you come back at ...?
¿Puede volver a ...?
pwehdeh bolbair a

TELEPHONING

Can I use your phone?
¿Puedo llamar por teléfono desde aquí?
pwehdo yamar por telefono dezdeh akee

Hello, can I speak to ...?
¿Puedo hablar con ...?
pwehdo ablar kon

> **Un momento.**
> *oon momento*
> Just a minute.

> **¿De parte de quién?**
> *deh parteh deh k-yen*
> Who's calling?

> **¿Dígame?**
> *deegameh*
> Hello.

> **Al habla/sí, soy yo.**
> *al abla/see soy yo*
> Speaking.

> **No está.**
> *no esta*
> He/she's not in.

Can I leave a message?
¿Podría dejar un recado?
podree-a deHar oon rekado

Please tell him that ... called.
Por favor, dígale que ha llamado ...
por favor deegaleh keh a yamado

I'm at ....
Estoy en ...
estoy en

My phone number is ...
Mi número de teléfono es el ...
mee noomero deh telefono es el

Can you ask him/her to call me back?
¿Puede decirle que me llame?
pwehdeh detheerleh keh meh yameh

YOU'LL SEE

Descuelgue el auricular.
deskwelgeh el owreekoolar
Lift the receiver.

Espere a oír el tono de marcar.
espaireh a o-eer el tono deh markar
Wait until you hear the dialling tone.

Introduzca las monedas.
eentrodoothka las monehdas
Insert coins.

Marque el número.
markeh el noomairo
Dial number.

Llamadas locales, nacionales e internacionales.
yamadas lokales nath-yonales eh eentairnath-yonales
Local, national and international calls.

Locutorio.
lokootor-yo
Payphones (either state or privately run).

THANKS

Thank you.
Gracias.
grath-yas

Thanks a lot, thank you very much.
Muchas gracias.
moochas grath-yas

> **¡De nada!**
> *deh nada*
> You're welcome!

> **¡No hay de qué!**
> *no i deh keh*
> Don't mention it!

That's very kind of you.
Muy amable.
mwee amableh

No thanks, no thank you.
No, gracias.
no grath-yas

Not for me thanks.
Para mí no, gracias.
para mee no grath-yas

Thank you for everything.
Gracias por todo.
grath-yas por todo

Many thanks for your help.
Muchas gracias por su ayuda.
moochas grath-yas por soo a-yooda

Could you thank him/her for me?
Dale/déle las gracias de mi parte.
daleh/dehleh las grath-yas deh mee parteh

He/she sends his/her thanks.
Me encargó que te/le diera las gracias.
meh enkargo keh teh/leh d-yehra las grath-yas

136

THEFT

My ... has been stolen.
Me han robado el/la ...
meh an robado el/la ...

Our room has been broken into.
Nos han entrado en la habitación.
nos an entrado en la abeetath-yon

Our car has been broken into.
Nos han forzado la cerradura del coche.
nos an forthado la thairradoora del kocheh

Can you cancel my credit cards for me?
¿Me puede anular las tarjetas de crédito?
meh pwehdeh anoolar las tarHehtas deh krehdeeto

All my money has gone.
Me ha desaparecido todo el dinero.
meh a desaparetheedo todo el deenehro

It was on the table/in the wardrobe/in my pocket.
Estaba encima de la mesa/en el armario/en el bolsillo.
estaba entheema deh la mehsa/en el armar-yo/en el bolseeyo

I was only out for a couple of minutes.
Salí un momento nada más.
salee oon momento nada mas

¿Puede describirlo?
pwehdeh deskreebeerlo
Can you describe it?

¿Vale/valía mucho?
baleh/balee-a moocho
Is/was it valuable?

Documentación, por favor.
dokoomentath-yon por favor
Can I see your papers please?

THIS AND THAT

English THIS is translated by Spanish **este** and its various forms. THAT is translated by **ese** or **aquel**.

Ese is used to refer to something near to the person being spoken to. **Aquel** is used to refer to something further away.

These words, called 'demonstratives' are like other adjectives in that they agree with the noun they qualify. But they come in front of the noun. The forms are:

m. sing.	**este**	**ese**	**aquel**
f. sing.	**esta**	**esa**	**aquella**
m. plur.	**estos**	**esos**	**aquellos**
f. plur.	**estas**	**esas**	**aquellas**

Este hotel. **Ese hombre.** **Aquellas furgonetas.**
esteh otel *eseh ombreh* *akeh-yas foorgonehtas*
This hotel. That man. Those vans (over there).

If you want to say THIS ONE or THAT ONE or THOSE THERE etc you use the same words as listed above (but they are written with an accent):

éste **ése** **aquél**
this one that one that one (over there)

There is also a neuter form which is used when no particular noun is being referred to (and so the question of masculine or feminine does not apply):

esto **eso** **aquello**

¿Qué es eso?
keh es eso
What is that?

No entiendo esto.
no ent-yendo esto
I don't understand this.

138

TICKETS

Two tickets for the pool please.
¿Me da dos tíques para la piscina?
meh da dos teekes para la peestheena

Can I book two tickets for tomorrow night?
¿Podría reservar dos localidades para mañana por la noche?
podree-a resairbar dos lokaleedades para man-yana por la nocheh

I'd like two singles to . . .
Quería dos billetes de ida a . . .
kehree-a dos beeyehtes deh eeda a

I'd like a return to . . .
Quería un billete de ida y vuelta a . . .
kehree-a oon beeyehteh deh eeda ee bwelta a

> **¿Para cuándo quiere la vuelta?**
> *para kwando k-yehreh la bwelta*
> When are you coming back?

> **¿Primera o segunda?**
> *preemaira o segoonda*
> First class or second?

For coming back the same day.
Para volver en el día.
para bolbair en el dee-a

I'm/we're coming back in three days.
Para volver dentro de tres días.
para bolbair dentro deh tres dee-as

I'd like to change this ticket and travel on Tuesday.
¿Me podría cambiar este billete por uno para el martes?
meh podree-a kamb-yar esteh beeyehteh por oono para el martes

TIME

(*see also DAYS*)

What's the time?
¿Qué hora es?
keh ora es

Excuse me, could you tell me what time it is?
Por favor, ¿me puede decir qué hora es?
por favor meh pwehdeh detheer keh ora es

It's one o'clock.
Es la una.
es la oona

It's ten past two.
Son las dos y diez.
son las dos ee d-yeth

It's a quarter past three.
Son las tres y cuarto.
son las tres ee kwarto

It's twenty-five past four.
Son las cuatro y veinticinco.
son las kwatro ee baynteetheenko

It's half past five.
Son las cinco y media.
son las theenko ee mehd-ya

It's twenty to six.
Son las seis menos veinte.
son las says mehnos baynteh

It's quarter to seven.
Son las siete menos cuarto.
son las s-yehteh mehnos kwarto

It's five to eight.
Son las ocho menos cinco.
son las ocho mehnos theenko

It's just after nine.
Son las nueve pasadas.
son las nwehbeh pasadas

It's just coming up to ten o'clock.
Van a ser las diez.
ban a ser las d-yeth

It's around three o'clock.
Serán más o menos las tres.
sairan mas o mehnos las tres

It's eleven o'clock exactly.
Son las once en punto.
son las ontheh en poonto

At eleven o'clock in the morning/at night.
A las once de la mañana/noche.
a las ontheh deh la man-yana/nocheh

At what time?
¿A qué hora?
a keh ora

It's getting very late.
Se está haciendo muy tarde.
seh esta ath-yendo mwee tardeh

Early in the morning.
Por la mañana temprano.
por la man-yana temprano

In the early hours of the morning.
De madrugada.
deh madroogada

Late at night.
Bien entrada la noche.
b-yen entrada la nocheh

Do we have time?
¿Tenemos tiempo?
tenehmos t-yempo

There's plenty of time.
Hay tiempo de sobra.
i t-yempo deh sobra

Every two hours.
Cada dos horas.
kada dos oras

How long does it take?
¿Cuánto se tarda?
kwanto seh tarda

Half an hour.
Media hora.
mehd-ya ora

Five minutes.
Cinco minutos.
theenko meenootos

Ages.
Un siglo.
oon seeglo

TOILETS

Can I use your toilet?
¿Puedo pasar al lavabo?
pwehdo pasar al lababo

Where's the gents?
¿Dónde está el servicio de caballeros?
dondeh esta el sairbeeth-yo deh kaba-yehros

Where are the ladies?
¿Dónde está el servicio de señoras?
dondeh esta el sairbeeth-yo deh sen-yoras

I need to go for a pee.
Tengo que ir a hacer pis.
ten-go keh eer a athair pees

She's in the toilet.
Está en el servicio.
esta en el sairbeeth-yo

Can I have some toilet paper?
¿Me da papel higiénico?
meh da papel een-yeneeko

It won't flush.
La cisterna no funciona.
la theestairna no foonth-yona

Could you go and see if he's/she's all right?
¿Puede ir a ver si se encuentra bien?
pwehdeh eer a bair see seh enkwentra b-yen

Aseos.	**Servicios.**
aseh-os	*sairbeeth-yos*
Toilets.	Toilets.
Señoras.	**Caballeros.**
sen-yoras	*kaba-yehros*
Ladies.	Gents.

TRAINS

(*see also* TICKETS)

How much does the train to ... cost?
¿Cuánto cuesta el billete a ...?
kwanto kwesta el beeyehteh a

Is this train going to ...?
¿Va este tren a ...?
ba esteh tren a

Which platform is it for ...?
¿En qué andén es para ...?
en keh anden es para

Is this the right platform for ...?
¿Es éste el andén para ...?
es esteh el anden para

Do I have to change?
¿Tengo que hacer trasbordo?
ten-go keh athair trazbordo

Do we change here for ...?
Para ir a ... ¿tenemos que hacer trasbordo aquí?
para eer a ... tenehmos keh athair trazbordo akee

What's this station called please?
Por favor, ¿cómo se llama esta estación?
por favor komo seh yama esta estath-yon

When's the last train back to ...?
¿A qué hora es el último tren de vuelta para ...?
a keh ora es el oolteemo tren deh bwelta para

> **Taquilla.**
> *takeeya*
> Ticket office.

UNDERSTANDING PEOPLE

Pardon?, sorry?
¿Perdón?, ¿cómo dices/dice?
pairdon komo deethes/deetheh

Could you say that very slowly?
¿Podrías/podría decirlo muy despacio?
podree-as/podree-a detheerlo mwee despath-yo

Could you write that down?
¿Me lo puedes/puede escribir?
meh lo pwehdes/pwehdeh eskreebeer

I don't understand.
No entiendo.
no ent-yendo

What did he say?
¿Qué ha dicho?
keh a deecho

Could you interpret for me?
¿Me lo podrías/podría traducir?
meh lo podree-as/podree-a tradootheer

Yes, yes, I understand.
Sí, sí, entiendo.
see see ent-yendo

Do you understand what I'm saying?
¿Entiendes/entiende lo que digo?
ent-yendes/ent-yendeh lo keh deego

Oh, I see!
¡Ah, ya!
a ya

WEATHER

What's the weather like?
¿Cómo está el tiempo?
komo esta el t-yempo

It's a lovely day.
Hace un día estupendo.
atheh oon dee-a estoopendo

What a horrible day!
¡Qué día más malo!
keh dee-a mas malo

What's the forecast for tomorrow?
¿Cuál es el pronóstico para mañana?
kwal es el pronosteeko para man-yana

It's raining again.
Está lloviendo otra vez.
esta yob-yendo otra beth

It's going to rain.
Va a llover.
ba a yobair

It'll clear up later.
Escampará luego.
eskampara lwehgo

It's so incredibly hot.
Hace un calor de espanto.
atheh oon kalor deh espanto

It's very cold.
Hace mucho frío.
atheh moocho free-o

WISHES

I wish I could.
¡Ojalá pudiera!
oнala pood-yehra

Best wishes. (as written on card)
Un cordial saludo.
oon kord-yal saloodo

Give him/her my best wishes.
Dale/déle muchos recuerdos de mi parte.
daleh/dehleh moochos rekwerdos deh mee parteh

He sends his best wishes.
Me dio muchos recuerdos.
meh d-yo moochos rekwerdos

Have a good journey!
¡Buen viaje!
bwen b-yaнteh

Happy birthday!
¡Feliz cumpleaños!
fehleeth koompleh-an-yos

Happy Christmas!
¡Feliz Navidad!
fehleeth nabeedad

Happy New Year!
¡Feliz año nuevo!
fehleeth an-yo nwehbo

And to you too.
¡Igualmente!
eegwalmenteh

ENGLISH-SPANISH DICTIONARY

Cross-references in this dictionary are to the phrase and grammar sections in the preceding part of the book.

A

a un; una; *see ARTICLES*
about *(approx)*
    aproximadamente
above: above the door por
    encima de la puerta
abroad en el extranjero; *(go,
    move etc)* al extranjero
accelerator el acelerador
accent el acento
accept aceptar; *see
    ACCEPTING*
accident el accidente; *see
    CAR ACCIDENTS*
accommodation el
    alojamiento; *see ROOMS*
accompany acompañar
account *(bank)* la cuenta
    (bancaria)
ache el dolor
adaptor el adaptador
address la dirección
address book la libreta de
    direcciones
admission charge la
    entrada
adult el adulto
advance: in advance por
    adelantado
advertisement el anuncio
advise aconsejar
aeroplane el avión
afraid: I'm afraid (of) tengo
    miedo (de)
after después; after ...
    después de ...
afternoon la tarde; *see
    DAYS*
aftershave la loción para
    después del afeitado
afterwards después
again otra vez
against contra

age la edad
agency la agencia
agent *(car)* el concesionario
aggressive agresivo
ago: a week ago hace una
    semana
agree: I agree estoy de
    acuerdo; *see AGREEING*
AIDS el SIDA
air el aire
air-conditioning el aire
    acondicionado
air hostess la azafata
airline la compañía aérea
airmail: by airmail por
    avión
airport el aeropuerto; *see
    FLYING*
alarm la alarma
alarm clock el despertador
alcohol el alcohol
alive vivo
all: all Spanish men todos
    los españoles; all Spanish
    women todas las
    españolas; all the milk
    toda la leche; all day todo
    el día; that's all eso es
    todo
allergic to alérgico a
alleyway el pasaje
all inclusive todo incluido
allow permitir
allowed permitido
all right: that's all right está
    bien; *(it doesn't matter)* no
    importa
almost casi
alone solo
already ya
also también
alternator el alternador
although aunque
altogether en total

149

always siempre
a.m.: at 7 a.m. a las 7 de la mañana
ambassador el embajador, la embajadora
ambulance la ambulancia
America América
American americano; (*man*) el americano; (*woman*) la americana
among entre
amp:13-amp de 13 amperios
ancestor el antepasado
anchor el ancla *f*
ancient antiguo
and y
angina la angina de pecho
angry enfadado
animal el animal
ankle el tobillo
anniversary (*wedding*) el aniversario (de boda)
annoying molesto
anorak el anorak
another distinto; **another bottle** otra botella
answer la respuesta; (*verb*) responder
ant la hormiga
antibiotic el antibiótico
antifreeze el anticongelante
antihistamine el antihistamínico
antique: it's an antique es antiguo
antique shop la tienda de antigüedades
antiseptic el antiséptico
any: have you got any bread/eggs? ¿tiene pan/huevos?; **I don't have any** no tengo
anybody: can anybody help? ¿alguien puede

ayudar?; **anybody can ...** cualquiera puede ...
anyway de todas formas
apart from aparte de
apartment el apartamento
aperitif el aperitivo
apologize disculparse
apology la disculpa; *see* APOLOGIES
appalling infame
appendicitis la apendicitis
appetite el apetito
apple la manzana
apple pie la tarta de manzana
application form el impreso de solicitud
appointment la cita
approve of aprobar
apricot el albaricoque
April abril
architect el/la arquitecto
area la zona
arm el brazo
arrest detener
arrival la llegada
arrive llegar
art el arte *f*
art gallery la galería de arte
arthritis la artritis
artificial artificial
artist el/la artista
as (*since*) como; **as fast as** tan rápido como; *see* COMPARISONS
ashamed avergonzado
ashtray el cenicero
ask preguntar
asleep dormido
asparagus los espárragos
aspirin la aspirina
asthma el asma *f*
astonishing increíble
at: at the station en la estación; **at Carmen's** en

casa de Carmen; **at 5 o'clock** a las cinco
Atlantic el Atlántico
atmosphere (*in group*) el ambiente; (*weather*) la atmósfera
attractive atractivo
audience los espectadores
August agosto
aunt la tía
Australia Australia
Australian australiano; (*man*) el australiano; (*woman*) la australiana
Austria Austria
Austrian austríaco
automatic automático
autumn el otoño
awake despierto
awful horrible
axe el hacha *f*
axle el eje

B

baby el bebé
baby-sitter la baby-sitter
bachelor el soltero
back (*of body*) la espalda; **to come/go back** volver; **the back wheel/seat** la rueda trasera/el asiento trasero
backpack la mochila
bacon el beicon
bad malo
badly mal
bag la bolsa; (*suitcase*) la maleta
bake cocer en el horno
baker's la panadería
balance el equilibrio

balcony el balcón
bald calvo
Balearics las Baleares
ball (*small*) la pelota; (*large*) el balón
ball-bearings el rodamiento de bolas
ball-point pen el bolígrafo
banana el plátano
bandage la venda
bank el banco
bank manager el director de banco
bar el bar
barbecue la barbacoa
barber el barbero
barmaid la camarera
barman el bárman
basement el sótano
basket el cesto
bath el baño
bathing cap el gorro de baño
bathroom el cuarto de baño
bath salts las sales de baño
bathtub la bañera
battery la pila; (*car*) la batería
be ser; estar; *see BE*
beach la playa
beans las judías
beard la barba
bearing (*in car etc*) el cojinete
beautiful (*house, day*) bonito; (*person*) guapo; (*meal etc*) riquísimo; (*holiday*) estupendo
because porque
become hacerse
bed la cama; **single/double bed** la cama individual/de matrimonio; **to go to bed** acostarse
bed and breakfast la habitación más desayuno

bed linen la ropa de cama

bedroom el dormitorio

bee la abeja

beef la carne de vacuno

beer la cerveza

before antes; **before I leave** antes de marcharme; **before 10** antes de las diez

begin empezar

beginner el/la principiante

beginning el principio

behalf: on behalf of the company en representación de la empresa

behaviour el comportamiento

behind detrás (de)

beige beige

Belgian belga

Belgium Bélgica

believe creer

bell el timbre; *(church etc)* la campana

belong pertenecer

below debajo de

belt el cinturón

bend la curva

berth *(for yacht)* el amarradero; *(in ship)* la litera

beside al lado de

best: the best el/la mejor

bet la apuesta; *(verb)* apostar

better mejor

between entre

beyond más allá de

bicycle la bicicleta

bidet el bidet

big grande

bikini el bikini

bill la cuenta

bird el pájaro

biro *(m)* el bolígrafo

birthday el cumpleaños; *see* WISHES

biscuit la galleta

bit: a little bit un poquito

bite el mordisco; *(insect)* la picadura

bitter amargo

bitter lemon el bitter lemon

black negro

black and white blanco y negro

blackberry la mora

bladder la vejiga

blanket la manta

bleach la lejía

bleed sangrar

bless: bless you! ¡Jesús!

blind ciego

blinds las persianas

blister la ampolla

blocked *(pipe etc)* obstruido; *(road)* cortado

blond rubio

blood la sangre

blood group el grupo sanguíneo

blouse la blusa

blow-dry el secado a mano

blown *(fuse)* fundido

blue azul

boarding pass la tarjeta de embarque

boat el barco

body el cuerpo; *(car)* la carrocería

boil hervir

bolt el cerrojo; *(verb)* echar el cerrojo a

bomb la bomba

bone el hueso

bonnet *(car)* el capó

book el libro; *(verb)*

reservar
bookshop la librería
boot (*shoe*) la bota; (*car*) el maletero
border la frontera
born: I was born in 1970 nací en 1970
borrow tomar prestado
boss el jefe
both: both of them los dos
bottle la botella
bottle-opener el abrebotellas
bottom el fondo; (*of body*) el trasero; **at the bottom of the hill** al pié de la colina
bottom gear la primera (marcha)
bouncer el vigilante de seguridad, el gorila
bowl el cuenco
bow tie la pajarita
box la caja
box office la taquilla
boy el chico
boyfriend el novio
bra el sostén
bracelet la pulsera
brake el freno; (*verb*) frenar
brake drum el tambor de los frenos
brake fluid el líquido de frenos
brake lining la guarnición de los frenos
brake shoes las zapatas de freno
branch (*company*) la sucursal; (*tree*) la rama
brand (*of product*) la marca
brandy el coñac
brave valiente
bread el pan;

white/wholemeal bread el pan blanco/integral
break romper
break down averiarse
breakdown (*nervous*) la crisis nerviosa
breakdown service la reparación de averías
breakdown vehicle la grúa
breakfast el desayuno
breast el pecho
breastfeed amamantar
breathe respirar
breeze la brisa
brick el ladrillo
bridge (*over river etc*) el puente
brief breve
briefcase la cartera
bright claro
brilliant (*idea etc*) luminoso
bring traer
Britain Gran Bretaña
British británico
brochure el folleto
broke: I'm broke no tengo una perra
broken roto
broker (*insurance etc*) el agente
brooch el broche
broom la escoba
brother el hermano
brother-in-law el cuñado
brown marrón
bruise el cardenal
brush el cepillo
Brussels sprouts las coles de Bruselas
bucket el cubo
budget (*for holiday etc*) el presupuesto
buffet meal el buffet
building el edificio

bulb (*light*) la bombilla
bull el toro
bullfight la corrida (de toros)
bullfighter el torero
bullring la plaza de toros
bumper el parachoques
bungalow el bungalow
bunk beds las literas
buoy la boya
burn la quemadura; (*verb*) quemar
bus el autobús
business el negocio
business card la tarjeta
business trip el viaje de negocios
bus station la estación de autobuses
bus stop la parada de autobús
busy ocupado; (*streets etc*) concurrido
but pero
butcher's la carnicería
butter la mantequilla
butterfly la mariposa
button el botón
buy comprar
by por; **by car** en coche

C

cabbage la col
cabin (*ship*) el camarote
cable (*elec*) el cable
cable car el teleférico
café la cafetería
cagoule el chubasquero
cake la tarta; (*small*) el pastel
cake shop la pastelería
calculator la calculadora

calendar el calendario
call llamar
calm down tranquilizarse
Calor gas (*tm*) el gas butano
camera (*still*) la máquina de fotos; (*cinecamera*) la cámara
campbed la cama de campaña
camping el camping
campsite el camping
camshaft el árbol de levas
can (*tin*) la lata; **I/she can** puedo/puede; **can you ...?** ¿puedes/puede ...?; *see PERMISSION, PRESENT TENSE*
Canada Canadá
Canadian canadiense; (*man/woman*) el/la canadiense
canal el canal
cancel anular
candle la vela
canoe la piragua
can opener el abrelatas
cap (*hat*) la gorra
capital (*money*) el capital
capital (*city*) la capital
captain el capitán
car el coche
caravan la caravana
caravan site el camping de caravanas
carburettor el carburador
card (*game*) la carta; (*business*) la tarjeta; (*postcard*) la postal
cardboard el cartón
cardigan la chaqueta
car driver el/la automovilista
care: to take care of cuidar de
careful: be careful! ¡ten

154

cuidado!
car ferry el trasbordador
car hire el alquiler de automóviles
car keys las llaves del coche
car park el aparcamiento
carpet la alfombra; *(fitted)* la moqueta
car rental el alquiler de automóviles
carriage el vagón
carrot la zanahoria
carry llevar
carry-cot el capazo
car wash el lavado de coches
case *(suitcase)* la maleta
cash: to pay cash pagar en efectivo
cash desk la caja
cash dispenser el cajero automático
cassette la cassette
cassette player el cassette
castle el castillo
casual *(clothes)* de sport
cat el gato
catastrophe la catástrofe
catch coger; **which bus do I catch** ¿qué autobús cojo?
cathedral la catedral
Catholic católico
cauliflower la coliflor
cause la causa
cave la cueva
ceiling el techo
celebrate celebrar
celebration la celebración
cemetery el cementerio
centigrade centígrado; *see CONVERSIONS*
central heating la calefacción central
centre el centro
century el siglo

certificate el certificado
chain la cadena
chair la silla
chairlift la telesilla
chairman el presidente
chairperson el presidente, la presidenta
chambermaid la camarera (de habitaciones)
chance: by chance por casualidad
change *(small)* el dinero suelto; *(verb)* cambiar; *(clothes)* cambiarse; **to change trains** hacer trasbordo
changeable *(weather)* variable
Channel el canal de la Mancha
charge cargar
charter flight el vuelo chárter
chassis el chasis
cheap barato
cheat *(with money)* timar
check verificar
check-in el mostrador de facturación
cheers! ¡salud!
cheese el queso
chef el chef
chemist's la farmacia
cheque el cheque
cheque book el talonario de cheques
cheque card la tarjeta bancaria
cherry la cereza
chest el pecho
chestnut la castaña
chewing gum el chicle
chicken el pollo
chickenpox la varicela

child el niño, la niña

children's portion la media ración

chilled (*wine*) frío

chilly (*weather*) fresco

chin la barbilla

chips las patatas fritas

chocolate el chocolate; **milk chocolate** el chocolate con leche; **plain chocolate** el chocolate amargo; **hot chocolate** el cacao caliente

choke el aire

choose elegir

chop la chuleta

Christian name el nombre de pila

Christmas la Navidad; *see* WISHES

church la iglesia

cider la sidra

cigar el puro

cigarette el cigarrillo

cigarette lighter el encendedor

cinema el cine

circle el círculo; (*in cinema etc*) el anfiteatro

citizen el ciudadano

city la ciudad

city centre el centro

claim form el impreso de solicitud

clarify aclarar

class la clase; **first class** la primera; **second class** la segunda

classical music la música clásica

clean (*adjective*) limpio; (*verb*) limpiar

cleansing cream la crema limpiadora

clear claro

clever listo

client el cliente

cliff el acantilado

climate el clima

climber el escalador

climbing boots las botas de escalar

cloakroom (*coats*) el guardarropa

clock el reloj

close (*verb*) cerrar

closed cerrado

cloth el paño

clothes la ropa

clothes peg la pinza de la ropa

cloud la nube

cloudy nublado

club el club

clutch el embrague

coach el autocar; (*of train*) el vagón

coast la costa

coat el abrigo; (*jacket*) la chaqueta

coathanger la percha

cockroach la cucaracha

cocktail el cóctel

cocoa el cacao

coconut el coco

code (*dialling*) el prefijo; (*postal*) el código (postal)

coffee el café; **black coffee** el café solo; **white coffee** el café con leche

coin la moneda

Coke (*tm*) la coca-cola

cold frío; **it is cold** hace frío; (*illness*) el resfriado; **I've got a cold** tengo catarro

cold cream la crema (de belleza)

collar el cuello
colleague el/la colega
collect (*person, laundry etc*)
recoger
collection la colección;
(*mail*) la recogida
colour el color
colour film el carrete en color
comb el peine
come venir; **I come from
London** soy de Londres;
to come back volver;
come in! ¡adelante!; *see
PRESENT TENSE*
comfortable cómodo
commercial comercial
Common Market el
Mercado Común
compact disc el disco
compacto
company (*firm*) la empresa
company car el coche de la
empresa
compartment el
compartimento
compass la brújula
compensation la
indemnización
competitor el/la
concursante; **competitors**
(*in business*) la competencia
complain quejarse
complaint la reclamación
complicated complicado
compliment el cumplido
component el componente
comprehensive insurance
el seguro a todo riesgo
compulsory obligatorio
computer el ordenador
concert el concierto
concrete el hormigón
condenser el condensador
condition la condición

conditioner el suavizante
condom el preservativo
conductor (*orchestra*) el
director (de orquesta)
conference el congreso
conference room la sala de
congresos
confirm confirmar
confusing confuso
congratulations!
¡enhorabuena!
connecting rod la biela
connection el enlace
constipated estreñido
consulate el consulado
contact (*get in touch with*)
ponerse en contacto con
contact lenses las lentillas
contacts (*of person*) los
contactos
contraceptive el
anticonceptivo
contract el contrato
cook el cocinero; (*verb*)
guisar
cooker la cocina
cooking utensils los
utensilios de cocina
cool fresco
coolant el refrigerante
cooling system el sistema
de refrigeración
cooperation la colaboración
copy la copia
corkscrew el sacacorchos
corner el rincón; (*street*) la
esquina; (*football*) el
corner
cornflakes los copos de maíz
correct correcto
corridor el pasillo
cosmetics los cosméticos
cost (*noun*) el coste; (*verb*)
costar

cot la cuna
cotton el algodón
cotton wool el algodón (en rama)
couchette la litera
cough la tos; (*verb*) toser
country el país
countryside el campo
couple (*man and woman*) la pareja; **a couple of ...** un par de ...
course: of course por supuesto
cousin el primo, la prima
cow la vaca
crab el cangrejo
crafts la artesanía
cramp el calambre
crankshaft el eje del cigüeñal
crash el choque
crayfish la cigala
cream (*food*) la nata; (*cosmetic*) la crema
crèche la guardería
credit card la tarjeta de crédito
credit note el vale
crew la tripulación
crisps las patatas fritas (a la inglesa)
crockery la loza
cross (*verb*) cruzar
crossing (*by sea*) la travesía; (*pedestrian*) el paso de peatones
crossroads el cruce
crowd el gentío
crowded abarrotado
cruise el crucero
crutches las muletas
cry llorar
cucumber el pepino
cup la taza

cupboard el armario
currency la moneda
current account la cuenta corriente
curry el curry
curtain la cortina
custom la costumbre
customer el cliente
customs la aduana
cut cortar
cutlery los cubiertos
CV el curriculum
cycling el ciclismo
cyclist el/la ciclista
cylinder el cilindro
cylinder head gasket la junta de culata

D

dad el papá
damage estropear
damn! ¡cuerno!
damp húmedo
dance bailar; *see DANCING*
danger el peligro
dangerous peligroso
Danish danés
dare atreverse (a)
dark oscuro
dashboard el tablero de mandos
data processing el proceso de datos
date (*appointment*) la cita; (*time*) la fecha
daughter la hija
daughter-in-law la nuera
day el día; *see DAYS*
dead muerto
deaf sordo

deal el trato; **it'a a deal!**
¡trato hecho!
dealer (*for cars etc*) el
vendedor
dear (*expensive*) caro
death la muerte
debt la deuda
decaffeinated descafeinado
December diciembre
decide decidir
decision la decisión
deck la cubierta
deck chair la hamaca
deep profundo
degree (*measurement*) el
grado
delay el retraso
deliberately a propósito
delicious exquisito
demand la demanda
Denmark Dinamarca
dent la abolladura
dentist el/la dentista
dentures la dentadura
postiza
deodorant el desodorante
department store los
grandes almacenes
departure la salida
depend: it depends
depende
deposit (*as security*) la señal;
(*first payment*) la entrada
depressed deprimido
dessert el postre
develop (*film*) revelar
device el aparato
diabetic diabético
dialect el dialecto
dialling code el prefijo
diamond el diamante
diarrhoea la diarrea
diary la agenda
dictionary el diccionario

die morir
diesel (*fuel*) el gas-oil
diet la dieta
difference la diferencia
different distinto
difficult difícil
difficulty la dificultad
dining car el vagón-comedor
dining room el comedor
dinner la cena; **to have
dinner** cenar
dipped headlights la luz de
cruce
dipstick la varilla
direct directo
direction la dirección
director (*of company*) el
director, la directora
directory enquiries
información
dirty sucio
disabled minusválido
disappear desaparecer
disappointed decepcionado
disaster el desastre
disc brake el freno de disco
disco la discoteca
discount el descuento
disease la enfermedad
disgusting asqueroso
disinfectant el desinfectante
disk (*computer*) el disco
distance la distancia
distributor el distribuidor
district (*in town*) el barrio
disturb molestar
dive bucear; **to dive in**
zambullirse
divorced divorciado
do hacer; **what does he
do?** ¿a qué se dedica?;
that'll do nicely eso irá
bien
docks el muelle

doctor el médico, la médica
document el documento
dog el perro
doll la muñeca
donkey el burro
door la puerta
dormitory el dormitorio
double doble
double bed la cama de matrimonio
double room la habitación doble
down: down there allí abajo
down payment la entrada
downstairs abajo
draught la corriente
dream el sueño
dress el vestido; (*someone*) vestir; (*oneself*) vestirse
dressing gown la bata
drink la bebida; (*verb*) beber
drinking water el agua potable
drive conducir
drive shaft el árbol de mando
driver el conductor, la conductora
driving licence el permiso de conducir
drop la gota; **I dropped it** se me cayó
drug (*narcotic*) la droga
drunk borracho
drunken driving conducir en estado de embriaguez
dry seco; (*verb*) secar
dry-cleaner's la tintorería
duck el pato
durex (*tm*) el preservativo
during durante
dustbin el cubo de la basura
Dutch holandés

duty (*tax*) el impuesto
duty-free libre de impuestos
duty-free shop la tienda libre de impuestos
dynamo la dinamo

E

each cada; **how much are they each?** ¿cuánto cuesta cada uno?
ear la oreja; (*inner*) el oído
early temprano; (*too early*) pronto
earrings los pendientes
earth la tierra
east el este; **east of** al este de
Easter la Pascua
easy fácil
eat comer
economy la economía
economy class la clase turista
EEC la CEE
egg el huevo; **soft-boiled egg** el huevo pasado por agua; **hard-boiled egg** el huevo duro
egg cup la huevera
either ... or ... o ... o ...
elastic elástico
Elastoplast (*tm*) la tirita
elbow el codo
electric eléctrico
electric blanket la manta eléctrica
electricity la electricidad
else: something else otra cosa
elsewhere en otra parte
embarrassing violento

embassy la embajada
emergency la emergencia
emergency exit la salida de emergencia
empty vacío
end el final
engaged (*toilet*) ocupado; (*to be married*) prometido; (*phone*) comunicando
engine el motor; (*train*) la locomotora
England Inglaterra
English inglés; **the English** los ingleses
Englishman el inglés
Englishwoman la inglesa
enlargement la ampliación
enough bastante; **that's enough** ya basta
enter entrar en
entertainment (*shows etc*) los espectáculos
entrance la entrada
envelope el sobre
epileptic epiléptico
equipment (*for sport*) el equipo
especially especialmente
estimate (*of costs*) el presupuesto
Eurocheque el eurocheque
Eurocheque card la tarjeta de eurocheque
Europe Europa
European europeo
even (*number*) par; **even here/if** incluso aquí/si; **even slower** aún más despacio
evening la tarde; *see* HELLO
every cada; **every time** cada vez; **every day** todos los días; **every twenty**

minutes cada veinte minutos
everyone todos
everything todo
everywhere por todas partes
exaggerate exagerar
example el ejemplo; **for example** por ejemplo
excellent excelente
except excepto
excess baggage el exceso de equipaje
exchange cambiar
exchange rate el cambio
exciting emocionante
excuse me por favor; (*interrupting*) perdone; (*when passing etc*) con permiso
executive el ejecutivo, la ejecutiva
exhaust el tubo de escape
exhaust fumes los gases de escape
exhibition la exposición
exit la salida
expenditure el gasto
expenses los gastos
expensive caro
experience la experiencia
explain explicar
export exportar
exposure (*photo*) la exposición
exposure meter el fotómetro
express (*mail*) urgente
extension lead el cable alargador
eye el ojo
eyebrow la ceja
eyeliner el lápiz de ojos
eye shadow la sombra de ojos

F

face la cara
factory la fábrica
faint desmayarse
fair (*funfair*) la feria; (*trade*) la feria de muestras
fall caer(se)
false falso
family la familia
famous famoso
fan el ventilador; (*supporter*) el fan; (*football*) el hincha
fan belt la correa del ventilador
far (away) lejos
fare (*travel*) el billete
farm la granja
farmer el granjero
fashion la moda
fashionable de moda
fast rápido
fat (*noun*) la grasa; (*adjective*) gordo
father el padre
father-in-law el suegro
fault: it's my/his fault es culpa mía/suya
faulty defectuoso
favourite favorito
fax el fax
fear el miedo
February febrero
fed up: I'm fed up (with) estoy harto (de)
feel sentir; **I feel well/ill** me siento bien/mal; **I feel like . . .** me apetece . . .; *see* FEEL
feeling (*emotion*) el sentimiento; (*physical*) la sensación
felt-tip el rotulador
feminist feminista

fence la valla
ferry (*small*) la barca de pasaje; (*large*) el trasbordador
fever la fiebre
few: few tourists pocos turistas; **a few** unos cuantos
fiancé(e) el prometido, la prometida
field el campo
fight la pelea; (*verb*) pelear
fill llenar; **to fill in** (*form*) rellenar
fillet el filete
filling (*tooth*) el empaste
film la película
filter el filtro
financial financiero
find encontrar
fine la multa; (*adjective*) fino; (*adverb*) bien; **fine!** ¡bien!
finger el dedo
fingernail la uña
finish terminar
Finland Finlandia
Finnish finlandés
fire el fuego
fire brigade los bomberos
fire extinguisher el extintor
fireworks los fuegos artificiales
firm (*company*) la empresa
first primero; (*firstly*) en primer lugar
first aid los primeros auxilios
first class la primera
first floor el primer piso
first name el nombre (de pila)
fish el pez; (*as food*) el pescado
fishbone la espina

fishing la pesca
fishmonger's la pescadería
fit (*healthy*) en forma
fix (*a date, in position*) fijar; (*repair*) arreglar
fizzy con burbujas
flag la bandera
flash el flash
flash cube el cubo de flash
flat el piso; (*adjective*) plano; (*battery*) descargado; **to have a flat tyre** tener un pinchazo
flat rate el precio fijo; (*of pay*) el sueldo base
flavour el sabor
flea la pulga
flight el vuelo
flirt coquetear
floor el suelo; (*storey*) el piso
floppy disk el disco blando
florist's la floristería
flour la harina
flower la flor
flu la gripe
fluent: he's fluent in Spanish domina el español
fly la mosca; (*verb*) volar
fog la niebla
fog light el faro antiniebla
folk music la música folklórica
follow seguir
food la comida
food poisoning la intoxicación alimentaria
foot el pie; **on foot** a pie
football el fútbol
for para
forbidden prohibido
forehead la frente
foreign extranjero
foreigner el extranjero

foreign exchange las divisas
forest el bosque
forget olvidar
fork el tenedor; (*in road*) la bifurcación
form el impreso
fortnight: a fortnight quince días
fortunately afortunadamente
forward (*mail*) remitir al destinatario
foundation cream la crema base
fountain la fuente
four-star (*petrol*) la super
foyer el vestíbulo
fracture la fractura
frame (*of picture*) el marco
frames (*of glasses*) la montura
France Francia
free libre; (*of charge*) gratis
freezer el congelador
freight (*goods*) la mercancía
French francés
frequent frecuente
fresh fresco
Friday el viernes
fridge el frigorífico
friend el amigo, la amiga
friendly simpático
from: from Madrid to Alicante desde Madrid a Alicante; **this is from me** esto es de mi parte
front la parte delantera; **in front of** delante de
the front wheel/seat la rueda delantera/el asiento de delante
frozen (*food*) congelado
fruit la fruta
fruit juice el zumo
fry freír

frying pan la sartén
fuel el combustible
fuel tank el depósito
full lleno
full beam la luz larga
full board la pensión completa
fun: to have fun divertirse; **have fun!** ¡que te diviertas!
funeral el funeral
funnel (*for pouring*) el embudo
funny (*amusing*) gracioso; (*strange*) raro
furious furioso
furniture los muebles
further más allá
fuse el fusible
future el futuro

G

game el juego; (*meat*) la caza
garage el garaje; (*repairs*) el taller; (*petrol*) la gasolinera
garden el jardín
garlic el ajo
gas el gas
gasket la junta
gas permeable lenses las lentillas porosas
gastritis la gastritis
gauge el indicador de nivel
gay homosexual
gear la marcha
gearbox la caja de cambios
gear lever la palanca de velocidades
generous generoso
gentleman el caballero
gents (*toilet*) el servicio de caballeros

genuine auténtico
German alemán
German measles la rubéola
Germany Alemania
get (*fetch*) traer; **can you tell me how to get to …?** ¿me puede decir cómo se va a …?; **it's getting cold** está refrescando; **to get back** (*return*) volver; **to get in** (*car*) subir; **to get off** bajarse; **to get up** levantarse; **get out!** ¡fuera de aquí!
gift el regalo
gin la ginebra
girl la chica
girlfriend la novia
give dar; **to give back** devolver; *see PRESENT TENSE*
glad: I'm glad that … me alegro de que ..
glass el cristal; (*drinking*) el vaso
glasses las gafas
glove compartment la guantera
gloves los guantes
glue el pegamento
go ir; **to go in** entrar; **to go out** salir; **to go down** bajar; **to go up** subir; **to go through** pasar (por); **to go away** marcharse; **go away!** ¡largo de aquí!; **it's all gone** se terminó; *see PRESENT TENSE*
goat la cabra
God Dios
gold el oro
golf el golf
good bueno

goodbye adiós
good-looking guapo
goods las mercancías
goose el ganso
gorgeous estupendo; (*man, woman*) guapísimo
got have you got ...? ¿tiene ...?
government el gobierno
grammar la gramática
grandfather el abuelo
grandmother la abuela
grapefruit el pomelo
grapes las uvas
grass la hierba
grateful agradecido
gravy el jugo de carne
greasy grasiento
Greece Grecia
Greek griego
green verde
green card la carta verde
greengrocer's la frutería
grey gris
grilled a la parrilla
grocer's la tienda de comestibles
gross bruto
ground floor la planta baja
group el grupo
guarantee la garantía
guest el invitado
guesthouse la casa de huéspedes
guide el guía
guidebook la guía
guilty culpable
guitar la guitarra
gun el arma de fuego
gynaecologist el ginecólogo, la ginecóloga

H

habit la costumbre
hail (*ice*) el granizo
hair el pelo
hairbrush el cepillo del pelo
haircut el corte de pelo
hairdresser el peluquero, la peluquera
hair dryer el secador de pelo
hair spray la laca
half la mitad; **half a litre/day** medio litro/día; **half an hour** media hora
half board la media pensión
hall (*in house*) el jol
ham el jamón; (*boiled*) el jamón de York
hamburger la hamburguesa
hammer el martillo
hand la mano
handbag el bolso
handbrake el freno de mano
handkerchief el pañuelo
handle (*door*) el picaporte
hand luggage el equipaje de mano
handsome guapo
hanger la percha
hangover la resaca
happen suceder
happy contento; *see* WISHES
harbour el puerto
hard duro
hard lenses las lentillas
hardly a penas
hat el sombrero
hatchback el tres puertas; el cinco puertas
hate odiar
have tener; **I have to ...** tengo que ...; *see* PRESENT TENSE

hay fever la fiebre del heno
he él; *see PRONOUNS*
head la cabeza
headache el dolor de cabeza
headlights los faros
health la salud
healthy sano
hear oír
hearing aid el audífono
heart el corazón
heart attack el infarto
heat el calor
heater (*in room*) la estufa
heating la calefacción
heavy pesado
heel el talón; (*of shoe*) el tacón
height (*of person*) la estatura; (*of mountain*) la altura
helicopter el helicóptero
hello ¡hola!; *see ATTENTION, HELLO, TELEPHONING*
helmet (*for motorbike*) el casco
help la ayuda; (*verb*) ayudar; **help!** ¡socorro!
helpful (*object*) práctico; (*person*) servicial
her (*possessive*) su; *see POSSESSIVES*; (*object*) la; le; *see PRONOUNS*
herbs las hierbas
here aquí; **come here** venga aquí; **here you are** (*offering*) tome
hers el suyo, la suya; *see POSSESSIVES*
hiccups el hipo
hide esconder
high alto
highway code el código de circulación
hill la colina

hillwalking el montañismo
him le; él; *see PRONOUNS*
hip la cadera
hire: for hire se alquila(n)
hire purchase la compra a plazos
his su; **it's his** es el suyo/la suya; *see POSSESSIVES*
history la historia
hit golpear; (*hit record*) el éxito
hitchhike hacer autostop
hitchhiker el/la autostopista
hitchhiking el autostop
hobby el hobby
hold tener
hole el agujero
holiday las vacaciones; (*public*) el día festivo; **the summer holidays** las vacaciones de verano
Holland Holanda
home: at home en casa; **to go home** volver a casa
homemade casero
homesick: I'm homesick tengo morriña
honest honrado
honestly sinceramente
honey la miel
honeymoon el viaje de novios
hood (*of car*) la capota; (*of coat etc*) la capucha
hoover (*tm*) la aspiradora
hope esperar; **I hope so** eso espero; **I hope not** espero que no
horn (*of car*) el claxon
horrible horroroso
horse el caballo
horse riding la equitación
hospital el hospital

hospitality la hospitalidad
hot caliente; (*to taste*) picante
hotel el hotel
hot-water bottle la bolsa de agua caliente
hour la hora
house la casa
housewife el ama de casa
house wine el vino de la casa
hovercraft el aerodeslizador
how? ¿cómo?; **how are you?** ¿cómo estás?; **how are things?** ¿qué tal te va?; **how many?** ¿cuántos?; **how much?** ¿cuánto?
hub el cubo
hub cap el embellecedor
humour el humor
hungry: I'm hungry tengo hambre
hurry darse prisa; **hurry up!** ¡date prisa!
hurt doler; **it hurts** duele
husband el marido
hydraulic hidráulico
hydraulics la hidráulica

I

I yo; *see PRONOUNS*
ice el hielo
ice cream el helado
ice lolly el polo
idea la idea
idiot el/la idiota
if si
ignition el encendido
ignition key la llave de contacto
ignition lock el bloqueo del

encendido
ill enfermo
immediately inmediatamente
import importar
important importante
impossible imposible
improve mejorar
in en; **in 1960** en 1960; **in English** en inglés; **is he in?** ¿está?
inch la pulgada; *see CONVERSIONS*
included incluido
incredible increíble
independent independiente
indicator (*car*) el intermitente
indigestion la indigestión
industrial industrial
industry la industria
infection la infección
infectious infeccioso
information la información
information desk la información
injection la inyección
injured herido
injury la herida
inner tube la cámara de aire
innocent inocente
insect el insecto
insect bite la picadura
insect repellent la loción antimosquitos
inside (*in building, box etc*) dentro
insomnia el insomnio
instant coffee el café instantáneo
instructor el monitor
instrument el instrumento
insulating tape la cinta aislante

insurance el seguro
insurance policy la póliza de seguros
intelligence la inteligencia
intelligent inteligente
interest el interés; **I'm interested in ...** me interesa ...
interesting interesante
international internacional
interpreter el intérprete
intersection la intersección
introduce presentar
invitation la invitación
invite invitar; *see INVITING PEOPLE*
invoice la factura
Ireland Irlanda
Irish irlandés
Irishman el irlandés
Irishwoman la irlandesa
iron (*metal*) el hierro; (*for clothes*) la plancha; (*verb*) planchar
ironmonger's la ferretería
island la isla
it (*as object*) lo; **it is mine** es mío/mía
Italian italiano
Italy Italia
itch el picor

J

jack (*car*) el gato
jacket la chaqueta
January enero
jaw la mandíbula
jazz el jazz
jealous celoso
jeans los vaqueros
jellyfish la medusa

jeweller's la joyería
jewellery las joyas
Jewish judío
job el trabajo
jogging el footing
joint (*to smoke*) el porro
joke el chiste
journey el viaje; *see WISHES*
jug la jarra
juice el zumo
July julio
jump saltar
jumper el jersey
jump leads los cables puente de batería
junction el cruce
June junio
just: just two sólo dos; **I've just arrived** acabo de llegar; **just around the corner** a la vuelta de la esquina

K

keep guardar
kerb el bordillo
key la llave
key ring el llavero
kidneys los riñones
kill matar
kilo el kilo; *see CONVERSIONS*
kilometre el kilómetro; *see CONVERSIONS*
kind amable; (*type*) el tipo
king el rey
kiss el beso; (*verb*) besar
kitchen la cocina
knee la rodilla
knife el cuchillo

knit hacer punto
knock golpear; (on door) llamar con los nudillos
knock over tirar; (car) atropellar
know saber; (person, place etc) conocer; **I don't know** no sé
knowledge el conocimiento

L

label la etiqueta
ladder la escalera de mano
ladies (toilet) el servicio de señoras
lady la señora
lager la cerveza
lake el lago
lamb el cordero
lamp la lámpara
lamppost la farola
land la tierra; (verb) aterrizar
landscape el paisaje
lane (alleyway) el callejón; (on motorway) el carril; (small road in country) el camino
language el idioma
language school la escuela de idiomas
large grande
last último; **last year** el año pasado; **at last** por fin
late tarde; **to arrive late** llegar tarde
later más tarde
laugh reír
launderette la lavandería automática
laundry (to wash) la ropa

sucia; (place) la lavandería
law la ley
lawn el césped
lawyer el abogado
laxative el laxante
lazy perezoso
lead (road) conducir
lead-free sin plomo
leaf la hoja
leaflet el folleto
leak la gotera
learn aprender
least: at least por lo menos
leather (hide, for clothes) el cuero; (shoes, bags) la piel
leave (go away) irse; (bag etc) dejar; (forget) dejarse
left izquierdo; **on the left (of)** a la izquierda (de)
left-hand drive la conducción por la izquierda
left-handed zurdo
left luggage la consigna
leg la pierna
lemon el limón
lemonade la gaseosa
lemon tea el té con limón
lend prestar
length el largo
lens el objetivo
less menos
lesson la clase
let (allow) dejar
letter la carta
letterbox el buzón
lettuce la lechuga
level crossing el paso a nivel
lever la palanca
library la biblioteca
licence el permiso
lid la tapa
lie (say untruth) mentir
lie down tumbarse

life la vida
life belt el salvavidas
life guard el vigilante
life jacket el chaleco salvavidas
lift (*elevator*) el ascensor; **to give a lift to** llevar en el coche
light la luz; (*on car*) el faro; **have you got a light?** ¿tiene fuego?; (*adjective*) ligero; **light blue** azul claro; (*verb*) encender
light bulb la bombilla
lighter el encendedor
lighthouse el faro
light meter el fotómetro
lightning el relámpago
like: I like ... ... me gusta; I would like querría; (*as*) como; *see LIKES*
lilo la colchoneta inflable
lip el labio
lipstick la barra de labios
liqueur el licor
list la lista
listen escuchar
litre el litro; *see CONVERSIONS*
litter la basura
litterbin la papelera
little pequeño; **a little bit of** un poquito de
live vivir
liver el hígado
living room la sala de estar
lizard la lagartija
load (*on lorry etc*) la carga
loan el préstamo
lobster el bogavante
lock la cerradura; (*verb*) cerrar con llave
locker (*at station etc*) la consigna automática

lollipop el chupa-chups (*tm*); (*ice*) el polo
lonely: to be feeling lonely sentirse muy solo
long largo
long-distance call la conferencia
long-term a largo plazo
loo el váter
look: to look at mirar; (*seem*) parecer; **to look like** parecerse a; **to look for** buscar; **look out!** ¡cuidado!; **I looked everywhere** miré por todas partes
loose (*nut, handle etc*) flojo
lorry el camión
lose perder
lost property office la oficina de objetos perdidos
lot: a lot mucho; **a lot of** mucho(s), mucha(s)
loud fuerte
lounge el salón
love el amor; (*verb*) querer; **to make love** hacer el amor
lovely encantador
low bajo
lubrication la lubricación
luck la suerte; **good luck!** ¡suerte!
luggage el equipaje
lukewarm tibio
lunch la comida
lungs los pulmones
Luxembourg Luxemburgo

M

macho viril
mad loco; (*angry*) furioso

magazine la revista
mail el correo
main principal
main road la carretera general
Majorca Mallorca
make hacer; **made of silver** de plata; **we'll never make it** *(getting to airport etc)* no vamos a llegar
make-up el maquillaje
male chauvinist pig el machista
man el hombre
manager el gerente
many muchos, muchas; **many people** mucha gente
map el mapa; *(of town)* el plano
March marzo
margarine la margarina
market el mercado
marmalade la mermelada de naranjas amargas
marriage el matrimonio
married casado
mascara el rímel
mass *(church)* la misa
match la cerilla; *(sport)* el partido
material la tela
matter: it doesn't matter no importa; **what's the matter?** ¿qué pasa?
mattress el colchón
May mayo
maybe tal vez
mayonnaise la mayonesa
me yo, me; **for me** para mi; **me too** yo también; **it's me** soy yo; *see PRONOUNS*
meal la comida; **enjoy your meal!** ¡buen provecho!

mean querer decir; *(person: with money)* roñoso
measles el sarampión; **German measles** la rubéola
measurements las medidas
meat la carne
mechanic el mecánico
medicine la medicina
Mediterranean el Mediterráneo
medium-sized de tamaño mediano; *(person)* de mediana estatura
meet encontrarse a
meeting la reunión
meeting place el punto de encuentro
melon el melón
member el miembro
membership card la tarjeta de socio
mend arreglar
menu la carta; **set menu** el plato del día
mess el lío
message el recado
metal el metal
metre el metro; *see CONVERSIONS*
midday el mediodía
middle el medio
midnight la medianoche
mild *(taste, weather)* suave
mile la milla; *see CONVERSIONS*
milk la leche
milkshake el batido
minced meat la carne picada
mind: do you mind if I ...? ¿le importa que ...?; **I don't mind** no me importa; *(don't mind which)* me da igual

nine el mío, la mía; *see POSSESSIVES*

mineral water el agua mineral

minute el minuto

mirror el espejo

Miss Señorita, Srta.

miss *(train etc)* perder; **I miss you** te echo de menos; **there's one missing** falta uno

mistake el error

misunderstand entender mal

misunderstanding el malentendido

mix mezclar

mixture la mezcla

model el modelo

modern moderno

moisturizer la crema hidratante

Monday el lunes

money el dinero

month el mes

monument el monumento

mood: in a good/bad mood de buen/mal humor

moon la luna

moped el vespino

more más; **I don't want any more** no quiero más; *see COMPARISONS*

morning la mañana; *see HELLO*

mosquito el mosquito

most of la mayoría de; *see COMPARISONS*

mother la madre

mother-in-law la suegra

motorbike la moto

motorist el/la automovilista

motorway la autopista

mountain la montaña

mountaineering el montañismo

mouse el ratón

moustache el bigote

mouth la boca

move mover; *(get something out of the way)* quitar

Mr Señor, Sr.

Mrs Señora, Sra.

much mucho; **not much** poco

multi-storey car park el aparcamiento de pisos

mum la mamá

muscle el músculo

museum el museo

mushrooms los champiñones

music la música; *(written)* la partitura

mussels los mejillones

must: I/you must ... tengo/tiene(s) que . . .; **you must not ...** no debe(s); *see NECESSITY*

mustard la mostaza

my mi; *see POSSESSIVES*

N

nail *(finger)* la uña; *(in wood)* el clavo

nail clippers el cortauñas

nailfile la lima (de uñas)

nail varnish el esmalte de uñas

nail varnish remover el quitaesmalte

naked desnudo

name el nombre; *see TALKING TO PEOPLE*

napkin la servilleta

nappy el pañal
narrow estrecho
national nacional
nationality la nacionalidad
natural natural
naturally naturalmente
nature la naturaleza
near cerca; **near...** cerca
de...; **near here/there**
cerca de aquí/allí; **the
nearest...** el... más
próximo/la... más próxima
nearly casi
neat (*drink*) solo; (*room,
appearance*) pulcro
necessary necesario; *see
NECESSITY*
neck el cuello
necklace el collar
need necesitar
needle la aguja
negative (*film*) el negativo
negotiate negociar
negotiations las
negociaciones
neighbour el vecino
neither...nor... ni... ni
...; **neither do I** yo
tampoco
nervous nervioso
net neto
neurotic neurótico
neutral (*gear*) el punto
muerto
never nunca
new nuevo
news la(s) noticia(s)
newsagent el kiosko de
prensa
newspaper el periódico
New Year el Año Nuevo; *see
WISHES*
next siguiente; **next year** el
año que viene; **next to** al

lado de
nice (*person*) simpático;
(*food*) rico; (*place*) bonito
nickname el apodo
niece la sobrina
night la noche; *see HELLO*
nightclub el night club
nightdress el camisón
nightmare la pesadilla
no no; **there is/are no...**
no hay...; *see
NEGATIVES*
nobody nadie
noise el ruido
noisy ruidoso
non-alcoholic sin alcohol
nonsense las tonterías
non-smoking no fumadores
no-one nadie
normal normal
north el norte; **north of** al
norte de
Northern Ireland Irlanda del
Norte
Norway Noruega
Norwegian noruego
nose la nariz
nosey fisgón
not no; *see NEGATIVES*
note (*money*) el billete
notebook el cuaderno
nothing nada
novel la novela
November noviembre
now ahora
nowhere en ningún sitio
number el número
number plate la matrícula
nurse la enfermera; (*male*)
el enfermero
nut (*to eat*) la nuez; (*for bolt*)
la tuerca

O

obnoxious odioso
obvious evidente
occasion la ocasión
occasionally de vez en
cuando
octane rating el octanaje
October octubre
octopus el pulpo
odd (*number*) impar;
(*strange*) raro
of de; *see ARTICLES*
off (*lights etc*) apagado
offer ofrecer
office la oficina
official oficial; (*noun*) el
funcionario
often a menudo
oil el aceite
oil change el cambio de
aceite
oil filter el filtro del aceite
oil pressure la presión del
aceite
ointment la pomada
OK vale; **I'm OK** estoy bien
old viejo; *see TALKING TO
PEOPLE*
old-age pensioner el/la
pensionista
old-fashioned de estilo
antiguo
old town la parte antigua (de
la ciudad)
olive la aceituna
olive oil el aceite de oliva
omelette la tortilla francesa;
potato omelette la tortilla
española
on encima de; (*lights etc*)
encendido; *see DAYS*
once una vez
one uno

onion la cebolla
only sólo
open (*adjective*) abierto;
(*verb*) abrir
opening times el horario de
apertura
opera la ópera
operation la operación
operator (*telephone*) la
operadora
opportunity la oportunidad
opposite lo contrario;
opposite the hotel
enfrente del hotel
optician el óptico
optimistic optimista
or o
orange la naranja; (*colour*)
naranja
orange juice el zumo de
naranja
orchestra la orquesta
order (*command*) ordenar;
(*commercially, meal*) pedir;
(*noun*) el pedido
organization la organización
organize organizar
original original
other otro
otherwise si no
our nuestro, nuestra; *see
POSSESSIVES*
ours el nuestro, la nuestra;
see POSSESSIVES
out fuera; **he's out** ha
salido
outside fuera; **outside ...**
fuera de ...
oven el horno
over (*above*) por encima de;
(*finished*) terminado; **over
there** (por) allá
overdone pasado
overnight (*stay, travel*) por la

noche
overtake adelantar
owe deber
own poseer; **my own car**
mi (propio) coche
owner el propietario, la
propietaria
oyster la ostra

P

pack hacer las maletas
package el bulto
package tour el viaje
organizado
packed lunch la bolsa con la
comida
packet (*of cigarette etc*) el
paquete
page la página; (*verb: person
in hotel etc*) avisar
pain el dolor
painful doloroso
painkiller el analgésico
paint la pintura; (*verb*)
pintar
paint brush (*artist's*) el
pincel
painting el cuadro
pair el par; **a pair of shoes**
un par de zapatos
palace el palacio
pancake la tortita
panic el pánico
panties las bragas
paper el papel
papers (*passport, driving
licence etc*) los documentos
paraffin la parafina
parcel el paquete
pardon? ¿cómo dice?
parents los padres

park el parque; (*verb*)
aparcar
parking lights las luces de
posición
parking place el parking
partner (*personal*) el
compañero, la compañera;
(*in business*) el socio, la socia
party (*celebration*) la fiesta;
(*group*) el grupo; (*political*)
el partido
pass (*mountain*) el puerto (de
montaña); (*verb*) (*hand,
move*) pasar; (*in car*)
adelantar
passenger el pasajero
passport el pasaporte
pasta las pastas alimenticias
pâté el paté
path el camino
patience la paciencia
patient: to be patient tener
paciencia
pavement la acera
pay pagar
payment el pago
payphone el teléfono
público
peach el melocotón
peanuts los cacahuetes
pear la pera
peas los guisantes
pedal el pedal
pedestrian el peatón
pedestrian crossing el paso
de peatones
pedestrian precinct la calle
peatonal
pen el bolígrafo
pencil el lápiz
pencil sharpener el
sacapuntas
penicillin la penicilina
penis el pene

enknife la navaja
people la gente
pepper (*spice*) la pimienta; (*vegetable*) el pimiento
per: per day por día; **per cent** por ciento
perfect perfecto
perfume el perfume
perhaps quizás
period el período
perm la permanente
permanent permanente
permit permitir
person la persona
personal personal
pessimistic pesimista
petrol la gasolina
petrol gauge el indicador de gasolina
petrol pump (*at garage*) el surtidor de gasolina; (*in car*) la bomba de gasolina
petrol station la gasolinera
petrol tank el depósito (de la gasolina)
phone telefonear
phone book la guía de teléfonos
phone box la cabina telefónica
phone number el número de teléfono
photocopy la fotocopia
photograph la fotografía; **to take a photograph of** fotografiar
photographer el fotógrafo
phrase book el libro de frases
pickpocket el/la carterista
pick up (*laundry, from airport etc*) recoger
picnic el picnic
picture (*on wall*) el cuadro;

(*photo*) la foto; (*drawing*) el dibujo
pie (*fruit*) la tarta
piece el trozo
pig el cerdo
pigeon la paloma
piles las almorranas
pile-up el accidente en cadena
pill la píldora
pillarbox el buzón (de correos)
pillow la almohada
pillow case la funda de almohada
pilot el piloto
pilot light el piloto
pin el alfiler
pineapple la piña
pink rosa
pins and needles: I've got pins and needles in my leg se me ha dormido la pierna
pipe la tubería; (*to smoke*) la pipa
piston el pistón
piston ring el aro de pistón
pity: it's a pity es una lástima
pizza la pizza
plain (*not patterned*) liso
plane el avión
plant la planta
plastic el plástico
plastic bag la bolsa de plástico
plate el plato
platform (*station*) el andén
play (*theatre*) la obra; (*verb*) jugar
pleasant agradable
please por favor
pleased contento; **pleased**

176

to meet you! ¡mucho gusto!

plenty: plenty of ... . de sobra; **that's plenty** basta y sobra

pliers los alicates

plug (*electrical*) el enchufe; (*in sink*) el tapón

plum la ciruela

plumber el fontanero

pm: at 4 p.m. a las 4 de la tarde; **at 10 p.m.** a las 10 de la noche

pneumonia la pulmonía

pocket el bolsillo

points (*in car*) los platinos

poison el veneno

poisonous venenoso

police la policía

policeman el policía

police station la comisaría

polite educado

political político

politics la política

polluted contaminado

pond el estanque

pool (*swimming*) la piscina

poor pobre; **poor quality** baja calidad

pop music la música pop

popular popular

pork la carne de cerdo

port (*drink*) el oporto

porter (*hotel*) el conserje

Portugal Portugal

Portuguese portugués

possibility la posibilidad

possible posible; *see POSSIBILITIES*

post: to post a letter echar una carta

postcard la tarjeta

poster (*for room*) el poster; (*in street*) el cartel

poste restante la lista de Correos

postman el cartero

Post Office Correos

potato la patata

poultry la carne de ave

pound (*money*) la libra (esterlina); *see CONVERSIONS*

powder (*for face etc*) los polvos

power cut el apagón

practical práctico

practise practicar

pram el cochecito

prawn la gamba

prefer preferir

pregnant embarazada

prepare preparar

prescription la receta

present (*gift*) el regalo; **at present** de momento

president (*of country*) el presidente, la presidenta

press (*newspapers*) la prensa

pretty bonito; **pretty good** bastante bueno

price el precio

price list la lista de precios

priest el cura

prince el príncipe

princess la princesa

print la reproducción; (*of photograph*) la copia

printed matter los impresos

prison la cárcel

private privado

probably probablemente

problem el problema

procedure el procedimiento

produce producir

product el producto

profit la ganancia

program(me) el programa

177

prohibited prohibido
promise la promesa; *(verb)*
   prometer
pronounce pronunciar
propeller shaft *(for boat)* el
   eje propulsor
prostitute la prostituta
protect proteger
protection factor el factor
   de protección
Protestant protestante
proud orgulloso
public público
publicity la publicidad
pudding *(dessert)* el postre
pull tirar
pump la bomba
puncture el pinchazo
pure *(gold, silk etc)* puro
purple morado
purse el monedero
push empujar
pushchair la sillita de ruedas
put poner; **where can I put
   my car?** ¿dónde puedo
   dejar el coche?
pyjamas el pijama

Q

quality la calidad
quarter la cuarta parte
quay el muelle
queen la reina
question la pregunta
queue la cola; *(verb)* hacer
   cola
quick rápido
quickly rápidamente
quiet tranquilo; **quiet!**
   ¡silencio!
quilt el edredón

quite bastante
quote *(from author)* la cita;
   (commercial) el precio

R

rabbit el conejo
race *(biological)* la raza;
   (sport) la carrera
radiator el radiador
radio la radio
rail: by rail en tren; *(send
   luggage etc)* por tren
railway el ferrocarril
rain la lluvia; *(verb)* llover;
   it is raining está lloviendo
rainbow el arco iris
raincoat la gabardina
rape la violación
rare poco común; *(steak)*
   poco hecho
rarely rara vez
rash *(on skin)* el sarpullido
raspberry la frambuesa
rat la rata
rate (of exchange) el
   cambio
rather bastante; **I'd rather
   ...** prefiero ...
raw crudo
razor la maquinilla de afeitar
razor blade la hojilla de
   afeitar
read leer
ready preparado
really realmente
rear lights las luces traseras
rearview mirror el (espejo)
   retrovisor
rear wheels las ruedas
   traseras
reason la razón

reasonable razonable
receipt el recibo
receive recibir
recently recientemente
reception (*hotel*) la recepción
reception desk la recepción
receptionist el/la recepcionista
recipe la receta
recognize reconocer
recommend recomendar
record el disco; (*sport etc*) el récord
record player el tocadiscos
red rojo; (*wine*) tinto
red-headed pelirrojo
red light district el barrio chino
reduction el descuento
refrigerator el refrigerador
refund devolver
registered mail el correo certificado
registration number el número de matrícula
regular regular
regulations las normas
relax relajarse
reliable de fiar
religion la religión
remember recordar; **I remember** recuerdo
rent el alquiler; (*verb*) alquilar
repair reparar
repeat repetir
reply la contestación
report el informe
representative (*of company*) el/la representante
reservation la reserva
reserve reservar
responsibility la responsabilidad

responsible responsable
rest (*remainder*) el resto; (*sleep*) el descanso; **to take a rest** descansar
restaurant el restaurante
return ticket el billete de ida y vuelta
rev counter el cuentarrevoluciones
reverse (*gear*) la marcha atrás
rheumatism el reúma
rib la costilla
rice el arroz
rich rico; (*food*) sabroso
ridiculous absurdo
right (*side*) derecho; **on the right (of)** a la derecha (de); (*correct*) correcto; **right here** aquí mismo; *see AGREEING WITH PEOPLE*
righthand drive la conducción por la derecha
right of way la prioridad
ring el anillo; (*on phone*) llamar por teléfono
ring road la carretera de circunvalación
ripe maduro
river el río
road la carretera
roadsign la señal de tráfico
roadworks las obras
rock la roca; (*music*) el rock
rock climbing la escalada
roll (*bread*) el bollo (de pan)
roof el tejado
roof rack la baca
room la habitación
room service el servicio de habitaciones
rope la cuerda
rose la rosa

rotten podrido
round (*circular*) redondo; *see* DRINKS
roundabout la glorieta
route la ruta
rowing boat la barca (de remos)
rubber la goma
rubber band la goma (elástica)
rubbish la basura; **rubbish!** ¡tonterías!; **these are rubbish** ¡menudas birrias!
rucksack la mochila
rude grosero
rug la alfombra
ruins las ruinas
rum el ron
run correr; (*buses, trains etc*) circular
rush hour la hora punta
rusty oxidado

S

sad triste
saddle la silla de montar
safe a salvo
safety pin el imperdible
sailboard la plancha
sailing la (navegación a) vela
sailing boat el balandro
salad la ensalada
salad dressing el aliño para la ensalada
salary el sueldo
sale la venta; (*reduced price*) la liquidación; **for sale** se vende
salesman el representante
salmon el salmón

salt la sal
salty salado
same mismo
sample la muestra
sand la arena
sand dunes las dunas
sandwich el bocadillo
sanitary towel la compresa
Saturday el sábado
sauce la salsa
saucepan el cazo
saucer el platillo
sauna la sauna
sausage la salchicha
savoury salado
say decir
scarf (*neck*) la bufanda; (*head*) el pañuelo (de cabeza)
scenery el paisaje
schedule: behind schedule retrasado; **we're on schedule** no vamos retrasados
school la escuela
science la ciencia
scientist el científico, la científica
scissors las tijeras
Scot (*man*) el escocés; (*woman*) la escocesa
Scotland Escocia
Scottish escocés
scrambled eggs los huevos revueltos
scream gritar
screw el tornillo
screwdriver el destornillador
sea el mar
seafood los pescados y mariscos
seagull la gaviota
search buscar; (*luggage*)

registrar
seasick mareado
seaside: at the seaside a orillas del mar
season la temporada; **in the high season** en la temporada alta
seasoning los condimentos
seat el asiento
seat belt el cinturón de seguridad
seaweed las algas
second segundo; (*in time*) el segundo
second class la segunda
second-hand de segunda mano
secret secreto
security la seguridad
see ver
seldom rara vez
selection la selección
self-service el autoservicio
sell vender
sellotape (*tm*) el celo
send enviar
sender el/la remitente
sensible razonable
sensitive sensible
separate separado
separately por separado
September se(p)tiembre
serious grave
serve servir; (*noun: tennis*) el saque
service el servicio
service charge el servicio
service station la estación de servicio
serviette la servilleta
several varios
sew coser
sex el sexo
sexist sexista

sexy sexy
shade la sombra
shampoo el champú
share compartir
shares (*financial*) las acciones
shark el tiburón
sharp (*knife*) afilado
shave afeitarse
shaving brush la brocha de afeitar
shaving foam la espuma de afeitar
she ella; *see PRONOUNS*
sheep la oveja
sheet la sábana
shell la concha
shellfish los mariscos
ship el barco
shirt la camisa
shock el susto
shock-absorber el amortiguador
shocking escandaloso
shoe el zapato
shoe laces los cordones de zapatos
shoe polish la crema de zapatos
shop la tienda
shop window el escaparate
shopping las compras; **to go shopping** ir de compras
shopping bag la bolsa de ir a la compra
shopping centre el centro comercial
shore la orilla
short corto
short circuit el cortocircuito
shortcut el atajo
shorts los pantalones cortos
short-sighted corto de vista

short-term a corto plazo

shoulder el hombro

shout gritar

show enseñar

shower la ducha; (*rain*) el chaparrón

shut (*adjective*) cerrado; (*verb*) cerrar

shutter (*photo*) el obturador

shutters (*window*) las contraventanas

shy tímido

sick: I feel sick no me encuentro bien; **I'm going to be sick** tengo ganas de devolver

side el lado

sidelights las luces de posición

sign (*roadsign*) la señal; (*notice*) el cartel; (*verb: write name*) firmar

signature la firma

silence el silencio

silencer el silenciador

silk la seda

silver la plata

silver foil el papel de aluminio

similar parecido

simple sencillo

since (*time*) desde (que); **since I've been here** desde que estoy aquí

sincere sincero

sing cantar

single (*unmarried*) soltero

single room la habitación individual

single ticket el billete de ida

sink (*go under*) hundirse; (*in kitchen*) el fregadero

sister la hermana

sister-in-law la cuñada

sit down sentarse

site (*camping etc, place*) el sitio

situation la situación

size (*clothes*) la talla; (*shoes*) el número

ski el esquí; (*verb*) esquiar

skid patinar

skiing el esquí

skin la piel

skin cleanser la leche limpiadora

skinny flaco

skirt la falda

skull el cráneo

sky el cielo

sleep dormir

sleeper el coche-cama

sleeping bag el saco de dormir

sleeping pill el somnífero

sleepy: I'm sleepy tengo sueño

slice la rebanada

slide (*photo*) la diapositiva

slim delgado

slippers las zapatillas

slippery resbaladizo

slow lento

slowly despacio

small pequeño

small change el dinero suelto

smell el olor; (*verb*) oler; **it smells** huele mal

smile la sonrisa; (*verb*) sonreír

smoke el humo; (*verb*) fumar; *see SMOKING*

smoking (*compartment*) fumadores

smooth (*texture, drink*) suave

snack el tentempié

snail el caracol

snake la culebra

sneeze estornudar
snore roncar
snow la nieve
so tan
soaking solution la solución limpiadora
soap el jabón
sober sobrio
soccer el fútbol
society la sociedad
sock el calcetín
socket el enchufe
sofa el sofá
soft blando
soft drink el refresco
soft lenses las lentes de contacto blandas
software el software
sole (of shoe) la suela; (of foot) la planta
solution la solución
some: some beer cerveza; some buttons unos botones
somebody alguien
something algo
sometimes a veces
somewhere en alguna parte
son el hijo
song la canción
son-in-law el yerno
soon pronto
sore: I've got a sore throat me duele la garganta
sorry perdón; I'm sorry lo siento; see APOLOGIES
soup la sopa
sour agrio
south el sur; south of al sur de
souvenir el (objeto de) recuerdo
spade la pala
Spain España

Spanish español
Spaniard (man) el español; (woman) la española
spanner la llave inglesa
spare parts las piezas de repuesto
spare tyre la rueda de repuesto
spark plug la bujía
speak hablar; do you speak ...? ¿habla usted ...?
specialist el/la especialista
speciality la especialidad
spectacle case la funda de gafas
spectacles las gafas
speed la velocidad
speed limit el límite de velocidad
speedometer el velocímetro
spell deletrear; how do you spell it? ¿cómo se escribe?; see ALPHABET
spend gastar
spice la especia
spider la araña
spinach las espinacas
spoke el radio
sponge la esponja
spoon la cuchara
sport el deporte
spot (on skin) el grano
sprain: I've sprained my ankle me he torcido el tobillo
spring (season) la primavera; (in seat etc) el muelle
square (in town) la plaza
stain la mancha
stairs las escaleras
stamp el sello
stand estar de pie; see DISLIKES

star la estrella
start empezar; **the car won't start** el coche no arranca
starter (*car*) el motor de arranque; (*food*) la entrada
state (*condition, political*) el estado
statement (*bank*) el extracto de cuenta
station la estación
stationer's la papelería
stay la estancia; (*remain*) quedarse; (*in hotel etc*) hospedarse
steak el filete
steal robar
steep empinado
steering la dirección
steering wheel el volante
stepfather el padrastro
stepmother la madrastra
steward el azafato
stewardess la azafata
sticky pegajoso
still (*adverb*) todavía; **keep still** no se mueva
Stock Exchange la Bolsa
stockings las medias
stomach el estómago; (*lower down: abdomen*) el vientre
stomach ache el dolor de estómago/vientre
stone la piedra
stop (*bus-*) la parada; (*verb*) parar; **stop!** ¡pare!
store (*put in storage*) guardar; (*shop*) la tienda
storey el piso
storm la tormenta
story la historia
straight ahead todo seguido
strange (*odd*) extraño

stranger el extraño, la extraña
strawberry la fresa
stream el arroyo
street la calle
stress el stress
strike la huelga
string la cuerda
stroke (*attack*) el ataque
strong fuerte
stuck: it's stuck (*coin etc*) está atascado; (*door, drawer etc*) está encajado
student el/la estudiante
stupid estúpido
suburbs las afueras
success el éxito
successful: he's successful tiene éxito; **were you successful?** ¿ha habido suerte?
suddenly de repente
suede el ante
sugar el/la azúcar
suggest sugerir; *see* SUGGESTIONS
suit el traje; **it suits you** te favorece
suitable adecuado
suitcase la maleta
summer el verano
sump el cárter
sun el sol
sunbathe tomar el sol
sunblock la crema solar de protección total
sunburn la quemadura solar
Sunday el domingo
sunglasses las gafas de sol
sunny soleado; **it's sunny** hace sol
sunrise el amanecer
sunset la puesta del sol
sunshine el sol

sunstroke la insolación
suntan el bronceado
suntan lotion la loción bronceadora
suntan oil el aceite bronceador
supermarket el supermercado
supper la cena
supplement el suplemento
supply proveer
support (*load, weight*) soportar
sure seguro
surname el apellido
surprise la sorpresa
surprising sorprendente
suspension (*of car*) la suspensión
swallow tragar
sweat sudar
sweater el jersey
Sweden Suecia
Swedish sueco
sweet el caramelo; (*to taste*) dulce
swim nadar
swimming la natación; **to go swimming** bañarse
swimming costume el bañador
swimming pool la piscina
swimming trunks el bañador
Swiss suizo
switch el interruptor
switch off apagar
switch on encender
Switzerland Suiza
swollen inflamado
synagogue la sinagoga
synthetic sintético

T

table la mesa; (*of figures*) la tabla
tablecloth el mantel
tablet la pastilla
table tennis el ping-pong
tail la cola
tailback la cola
take tomar; **to take away** (*remove*) llevarse; (*food*) para llevar; **to take off** (*plane*) despegar; (*clothes*) quitarse
talc los polvos de talco
talk hablar; (*lecture etc*) la conferencia
tall alto
tampon el tampón
tan el bronceado
tank el depósito
tap el grifo
tape (*cassette*) la cinta; (*sticky*) la cinta adhesiva
tape recorder la grabadora
target (*objective*) la meta
tart la tarta
taste el sabor; (*verb: try*) probar
tax el impuesto
taxi el taxi; *see TAXIS*
taxi driver el/la taxista
taxi rank la parada de taxis
tea el té
teabag la bolsita de té
teach: will you teach me some Spanish? ¿me podría enseñar algo de español?
teacher el profesor, la profesora
team el equipo
teapot la tetera
tea towel el paño de cocina

technical técnico
teenager el/la adolescente
telegram el telegrama
telephone el teléfono
telephone box la cabina telefónica
telephone directory la guía de teléfonos
television la televisión; **on television** en la televisión; **to watch television** ver la televisión
telex el télex
temperature la temperatura; (*medical*) la fiebre
temporary provisional
tennis el tenis
tent la tienda (de campaña)
terrible horrible
terrific estupendo
test examinar
than que; *see COMPARISONS*
thank agradecer; **thank you** gracias; *see THANKS*
that (*adjective*) ese, esa; (*pronoun*) ése, ésa; (*that over there*) (*adjective*) aquel, aquella; (*pronoun*) aquél, aquélla; **what's that?** ¿qué es eso/aquello?; **I think that ...** creo que ...; *see REFERRING TO THINGS*
the el, la; (*plural*) los, las; *see ARTICLES*
theatre el teatro
their su; *see POSSESSIVES*
theirs el suyo, la suya; *see POSSESSIVES*
them les, las; ellos, ellas; *see PRONOUNS*

then entonces
there allí; **there is/are ...** hay ...; **is/are there ...?** ¿hay ...?
thermometer el termómetro
thermos flask el termo
thermostat el termostato
these estos, éstos; *see REFERRING TO THINGS*
they ellos, ellas; *see PRONOUNS*
thick grueso
thief el ladrón
thin delgado
thing la cosa
think pensar
third party (*insurance*) el seguro contra terceros
thirsty: I am thirsty tengo sed
this (*adjective*) este, esta; (*pronoun*) esto; **this one** éste, ésta; *see REFERRING TO THINGS*
those (*adjective*) esos, esas; (*pronoun*) ésos, ésas; (*that over there*) (*adjective*) aquellos, aquellas; (*pronoun*) aquéllos, aquéllas; *see REFERRING TO THINGS*
thread el hilo
throat la garganta
throat lozenges las pastillas para la garganta
through por
throw tirar; **to throw away** tirar
thumb el pulgar
thunder el trueno
thunderstorm la tormenta
Thursday el jueves

ticket (*cinema etc*) la entrada; (*for travel*) el billete
ticket office la taquilla
tie la corbata
tight ajustado
tights (*thick*) los leotardos; (*sheer*) las medias panty
time el tiempo; **two/three times** dos/tres veces; **next time** la próxima vez; **on time** a la hora; **what time is it?** ¿qué hora es?; *see TIME*
timetable el horario
tin opener el abrelatas
tip la propina
tired cansado
tiring agotador
tissues los kleenex (*tm*)
to: to Madrid a Madrid; **to the bank** al banco
toast el pan tostado
tobacco el tabaco
today hoy
toe el dedo del pie
together juntos
toilet el servicio
toilet paper el papel higiénico
tomato el tomate
tomorrow mañana; *see DAYS*
tongue la lengua
tonight esta noche
tonsillitis las anginas
tonsils las anginas
too (*also*) también; **too fast** demasiado rápido; **not too much** no demasiado
tool herramienta
tooth el diente
toothache el dolor de muelas
toothbrush el cepillo de

dientes
toothpaste la pasta de dientes
top: at the top en lo alto
torch la linterna
touch tocar
tough (*meat*) duro; **tough luck** mala suerte
tour la visita turística; (*of castle etc*) la visita
tourist el/la turista
tow remolcar
towel la toalla
tower la torre
tow line el cable de remolque
town la ciudad
town hall el ayuntamiento
toy el juguete
tracksuit el chandal
trade union el sindicato
tradition la tradición
traditional tradicional
traffic el tráfico
traffic jam el embotellamiento
traffic lights el semáforo
traffic warden el guardia de tráfico
trailer (*behind car*) el remolque
train el tren
trainers los deportivos
transformer el transformador
transistor (*radio*) el transistor
translate traducir
translation la traducción
translator el traductor, la traductora
travel viajar
travel agent's la agencia de viajes
traveller's cheque el cheque de viaje

tray la bandeja
tree el árbol
tremendous fantástico
trip la excursión
trolley el carrito
trouble el apuro
trousers los pantalones
true verdadero; it's true es
verdad
truth la verdad
try intentar; to try on
probarse
T-shirt la camiseta
tube (*tyre*) la cámara
Tuesday el martes
tuna fish el atún
tunnel el túnel
turkey el pavo
Turkey Turquía
Turkish turco
turn girar; to turn off
(*driving*) torcer
tweezers las pinzas
twice dos veces
twin beds las camas gemelas
twins los gemelos
two-star (*petrol*) la normal
typewriter la máquina de
escribir
typical típico
tyre el neumático
tyre lever la palanca para
neumáticos
tyre pressure la presión de
los neumáticos

U

ugly feo
umbrella el paraguas
uncle el tío
under debajo de

underdone poco hecho
underground el metro
underneath (por) debajo;
underneath ... debajo de .
underpants los calzoncillos
understand entender
underwear la ropa interior
unemployed sin trabajo
unfortunately por desgracia
United States los Estados
Unidos
university la universidad
unleaded sin plomo
unpack deshacer las maletas
unpleasant desagradable
until hasta; until I ... hasta
que ...
unusual poco corriente
up: up there allí arriba
upside down boca abajo
upstairs arriba
urgent urgente
us nos, nosotros, nosotras;
see PRONOUNS
use usar
useful útil
usual habitual
usually normalmente

V

vacancy (*room*) la habitación
libre
vacation la vacación
vaccination la vacuna
vacuum cleaner la
aspiradora
vagina la vagina
valid válido
valley el valle
valuable valioso

valve la válvula
van la furgoneta
vanilla la vainilla
vase el jarrón
VAT el IVA
VD la enfermedad venérea
veal la ternera
vegetables las verduras
vegetarian vegetariano
vehicle el vehículo
very muy; **very much** mucho
vest la camiseta
vet el veterinario
via (pasando) por
video el vídeo
view la vista
viewfinder el visor
village el pueblo
vinegar el vinagre
vineyard la viña
visa el visado
visit la visita; *(verb)* visitar
vitamin las vitaminas
voice la voz
voltage el voltaje

W

waist la cintura
wait esperar; **wait for me!** ¡espérame!
waiter el camarero
waiting room la sala de espera
waitress la camarera
wake up *(someone)* despertar; *(oneself)* despertarse
Wales Gales
walk el paseo; *(verb)* andar; **to go for a walk** ir de paseo

walking boots las botas de marcha
walkman *(tm)* el cassette individual
wall la pared
wallet la billetera
want querer; **I want ...** quiero ...; **he wants ...** quiere ...; **do you want ...?** ¿quieres/quiere ...?; *see PRESENT TENSE*
war la guerra
warden *(hostel)* el celador, la celadora
warehouse el almacén
warm caliente; **it's warm** hace calor
warn advertir
warning la advertencia
warning triangle el triángulo de señalización
wash lavar; *(oneself)* lavarse
washbasin el lavabo
washer *(for bolt etc)* la arandela
washing: to do the washing lavar la ropa
washing machine la lavadora
washing powder el detergente (en polvo)
washing-up: to do the washing up fregar
washing-up liquid el lavavajillas
wasp la avispa
watch *(for time)* el reloj (de pulsera); *(take care of)* cuidar de; *(look at)* ver
water el agua *f*
waterfall la cascada
waterproof *(watch etc)* sumergible; *(clothes)* impermeable

waterski(ing) el esquí
acuático
wave (*in sea*) la ola; (*in hair*)
la onda
way: this way (*like this*) de
esta manera; **can you tell
me the way to the ...?**
¿me puede decir cómo se va
a ...?; *see DIRECTIONS*
we nosotros, nosotras; *see
PRONOUNS*
weak débil
weather el tiempo; *see
WEATHER*
weather forecast el
pronóstico del tiempo
wedding la boda
Wednesday el miércoles
week la semana
weekend el fin de semana
weight el peso
welcome! ¡bienvenido!;
you're welcome de nada
well bien; **he's well/he's
not well** se encuentra
bien/no se encuentra bien
well done (*meat*) muy hecho
wellingtons las botas de
goma
Welsh galés
Welshman el galés
Welshwoman la galesa
west el oeste; **west of** al
oeste de
wet mojado
what? ¿qué?; **what ...?**
¿qué ...?
wheel la rueda
wheelchair la silla de ruedas
when? ¿cuándo?
where? ¿dónde?
which? ¿cuál?
while mientras
whipped cream la nata

montada
whisky el whisky
whisper susurrar
white blanco
Whitsun Pentecostés
who? ¿quién?; **the
man/woman who** el
hombre/la mujer que
whole entero
whooping cough la
tosferina
whose: whose is this? ¿de
quién es esto?
why? ¿por qué?
wide ancho; **3 m wide** de 3
metros de ancho
wide-angle lens objetivo de
ángulo abierto
widow la viuda
widower el viudo
wife la mujer
wild (*flowers, fruits*) silvestre
will *see FUTURE*
win ganar
wind el viento
window la ventana
window seat el asiento de
ventanilla
**window-shopping: to go
window-shopping** salir a
ver escaparates
windscreen el parabrisas
windscreen washer el
lavaparabrisas
windscreen wiper el
limpiaparabrisas
windsurfing el windsurf
windy: it's windy hace
viento
wine el vino;
red/white/rosé wine el
vino tinto/blanco/rosado
wine list la carta de vinos
wing el ala *f*; (*car*) la aleta

wing mirror el espejo retrovisor
winter el invierno
winter sports los deportes de invierno
wire el alambre; *(electric)* el cable
wiring diagram el esquema de conexiones
wish: best wishes saludos; *see WISHES*
with con; **with me** conmigo
without sin
witness el/la testigo; *see CAR ACCIDENTS*
woman la mujer
wonderful maravilloso
wood la madera
woods el bosque
wool la lana
word la palabra
work el trabajo; *(verb)* trabajar; **it's not working** no funciona
works *(factory etc)* los talleres
world el mundo
worry la preocupación; **don't worry** no se preocupe
worse peor
worst: the worst ... el/la peor ...; **the worst that ...** lo peor que ...
wrap envolver
wrapping paper el papel de envolver
wrench la llave inglesa
wrist la muñeca
write escribir
write-off: it's a write-off está para la chatarra
writing paper la cuartilla
wrong: he's wrong está equivocado; **the wrong**

key la llave que no es; **I took the wrong key** me he equivocado de llave

X

X-ray la radiografía

Y

yacht el yate
year el año
yellow amarillo
yellow pages las páginas amarillas
yes sí
yesterday ayer; *see DAYS*
yet: not yet todavía no
yoghurt el yogur
you usted; *(familiar)* tú; *(plural)* ustedes; *(familiar)* vosotros, vosotras *see PRONOUNS*
young joven
your su; *(familiar)* tu; *(familiar plural)* vuestro, vuestra; *see POSSESSIVES*
yours el suyo, la suya; *(familiar)* el tuyo, la tuya; *see POSSESSIVES*
youth hostel el albergue juvenil

Z

zero cero
zip la cremallera
zoo el zoo
zoom lens el zoom